AUTHOR JOURNEY

SUCCESS

7 STEPS

TO YOUR

BESTSELLING BOOK

BY

AMELIA GRIGGS

Paperback ISBN: 978-1-7330666-6-2

Independently Published by Amelia Griggs, Green Ridge Press

Green Ridge Press

Cover design by Debbie O'Byrne, JetLaunch

Table of Contents

Dedication 6

Thank You and Gratitude 7

About This Book 9

BONUS! FREE GIFT! 13

Step 1: Foundation and Goals 17

    Establish a Strong Foundation 17

    Start Your Journey.. 19

    My Journey Thoughts... 23

    Define Measurable Goals.. 28

    Select Your Genre or Topic 32

Step 2: The Writing Process 35

    Do What You Love.. 35

    What If You Don't Love to Write................................. 35

    Let's Begin 35

    Writing Tools and Methods 37

    The Method I Used For This Book............................... 38

    Create a Writing Oasis 40

    Electronic vs. Handwriting – What's Better?.............. 41

    Writing in the Middle of the Night?............................ 41

    Reduce Distractions, Noise and Stress and Increase Writing Time 42

    Motivational Quotes 43

    Final Thoughts When Writing 44

Step 3: Learning, Doing Your Homework and Pre-Marketing 47

    Learning How to Be Successful – Turning Negativity into Positivity 47

    Doing Your Homework.. 50

Get Active Online 51

Attend Classes and Workshops... 51

Do Your Book Research 52

Book Categories 52

Keywords... 54

Pre-Marketing 55

Build Your Brand 55

Social Media - Create an Online Presence 56

Pre-Order Options 56

Step 4: Author Networking 61

Networking Ideas 61

Networking With Other Authors.. 61

Sign-Up for Author Events 62

Share Information 62

Build a Book Launch Team 63

Authors Helping Authors - Interviews 64

Other Networking 63

Step 5: The Formatting and Editing Process 93

The Formatting Process 93

Refining Your Outline.. 94

Layout of Pages for Print Version (Paperback or Hardcover) 97

Using Page Breaks 98

Creating an Interactive Table of Contents 99

The Editing Process 102

Editing and Proofing – Do it Yourself or Hire Someone?........... 102

Spelling and Grammar Check... 103

Final Proofing and Read Out Loud Tools.................................. 104

Your Book Cover...105

Step 6: The Publishing Process 113

Publishing Options 113

Why Self-Publishing? 114

Putting It All Together with KDP 115

Let's Talk About Kindle Direct Publishing 115

Preparing Your Manuscript for Print Versions vs. eBook Format.............116

Fixed Layout Format vs. Reflowable File Format (eBooks).......................117

File Format Options For Uploading an eBook on KDP 118

Kindle Create...119

Kindle Previewer 122

Other Ways to Preview Your eBook and Paperback...................122

Uploading Your Paperback Book on KDP................................123

Uploading Your eBook on KDP...127

Step 7: The Book Launch and Beyond 133

The Launch Process...133

Advanced Review Copy (ARC) Strategy 134

Do a Soft Launch 136

It's Time to Publish! 137

The Official Launch...138

10 Simple Things To Do to Promote Your Book......................139

Resources...141

More Books in The Author Journey Success Toolkit Series 143

Dedication

To my husband, and children, and everyone in my family.

To all my friends near and far.

To every author I know.

Your faith in me and ongoing support gave me the courage to write this book.

Thank You and Gratitude

To my greatest teacher, my Mother, for telling me stories, teaching me how to be grateful, and igniting my creative energy. You truly inspired me to write, design and create just about anything. Thank you for helping me appreciate every little thing in our wonderful world. And most important, for always telling me to tell myself "I can do it". No matter what it was, you helped me believe that I could.

To my second-grade teacher, Miss Zavrel, for making me feel special instead of awkward, and loved instead of forgotten. Sometimes it is the smallest actions which cause the biggest positive impact in someone's life. Although your face is but a faint memory, I will remember you always.

To Ronnie Dauber and Betsy A. Riley, for giving aspiring authors the opportunity to see our short stories published in a real book for the first time. Once I saw my first short story in a printed book, I was hooked, and I knew I was destined to write more.

To Ali, Hallie, Carol, Barb, Karen, Rita, Andrea and Melissa, and everyone in the SCBWI Writer's Critique Group, for allowing me to be part of your group, and for critiquing my children's stories.

To Steve Scott, Barrie Davenport and Ron Clendenin, for creating Authority Pub Academy. Your course helped me forge ahead when I didn't know where to begin.

To Sarah Lentz, for answering my questions when I needed help, and for all your support.

To Corinne Hewitt, for all your advice and support. Sometimes even if you are countries apart, you find someone who is dear to your heart.

To Ellwyn Autumn, for being my story time buddy back in the day, and for all your support.

Special thanks to the authors in the Authors Helping Authors section of this book, who shared their experience in author interviews.

To all author groups and associated members out there, both in person and online, for the experiences and information you share every day.

About This Book

HOW TO USE THIS BOOK

If you have always wanted to harness your love of writing and publish a book, you are in the right place. The intent of this book is to not only share my writing and self-publishing journey with you, but to help you in your journey as well. As a wife, mother, freelance Instructional Designer and eLearning Developer, as well as an online blogger and writer, I want to assure you that it's definitely possible to write and self-publish a book while working full-time. Over the course of five years, from 2015 through 2020, I wrote and self-published nine books. By the time this book and the whole *Author Journey Success Toolkit* series is completed in 2021, I will have approximately 14 books under my belt and counting. Beyond that, the possibilities are limitless. All you need is drive, commitment and discipline, along with faith, determination, and confidence. With all those things, along with a thirst for learning, anything is possible.

Throughout this book, I include practical steps to take to successfully plan, outline, write, publish, and market your book; however, more importantly, I include strategies I used (and still use) to help me with time management, daily routines and having the right mindset.

Author Journey Success – 7 Steps to Your Bestselling Book, along with all other books and materials in the *Author Journey Success Toolkit* series is based on my journal of notes for the past five years. During my journey of writing, self-publishing and marketing nine books, in three different book series, in two different genres, including 80 instructional videos, I wrote down everything I did in the process for a period of five years. I did this to help me remember what I did, and to help me figure out how I could do it better the next time.

This book is more than just the steps on how to write, publish and market books. It is a roadmap to success, including a journey of ups and downs that I encountered along the way.

There is a lot of material covered, and in some cases, there are links to articles and videos I have put together to further demonstrate processes and techniques.

If you have already started writing a book and you are considering self-publishing but need help moving forward, this book can help you get there. In this case, you may want to browse through the table of contents to select specific topics to help you along your journey.

If you're not sure whether you want to self-publish your book or pursue traditional publishing, you will learn about different publishing options as well as why I choose to self-publish.

Maybe you have been writing for years and don't know where to begin. Maybe you wrote a book years ago and you are not sure about the next step. Maybe you tried pitching to agents for years in an effort to traditionally publish, and now you are burnt out and tired of waiting for the publishing fairy to magically create your book. Perhaps you have always had a dream of writing a book and becoming a published author. Whatever your dream may be, whether it is to write a novel, a memoir, a self-help book, a training guide, or a children's book, I'd like to try to help you get there. My wish is for you to use the information in this book as a springboard to your success.

"Let no feeling of discouragement prey upon you, and in the end, you are sure to succeed."

~Abraham Lincoln

WHAT'S INCLUDED IN THIS BOOK

There are seven steps in this book. Each step is broken up into smaller sections to make the information bite-sized, and easy to absorb. Just like a large meal, if you take in too much at once, you will feel stuffed; instead, if you take it slow and take in a little bit at a time, it's a lot easier to digest. Like many of my books, I designed this book with the modern learner in mind. Short bursts of information are simpler to comprehend and easier to remember.

Also included throughout the chapters are easy-to-follow action items and mini-exercises to help you keep track of your progress.

This book has a dual purpose: First, it will explain to you firsthand, what it was like for me as I embarked on the exciting world of writing and becoming an author, and how I successfully wrote, designed and published nine books in two different genres while working full-time; second, it will provide the support, inspiration and information you need to get started on your own successful journey.

You can complete each step at your own pace. Remember to bookmark sections which you need to refer back to during your journey.

You may notice visuals used throughout this book and related books, workbooks, and journals in the series, which indicate interactive activities and different phases of the journey. Here are some of the icons used throughout this book.

Goal Setting	Brainstorming	Activity/Exercise	Writing
Learning	Networking	Designing	Milestone
Publishing	Launching	Marketing	Nourishing

BONUS! FREE GIFT!

To thank you for purchasing this book, you will receive *The Author Journey Success Roadmap!*

Two Ways to Download Your Free Gift:

Visit Landing Page Here:
geni.us/author-roadmap
or
Visit Product Page:
ameliagriggs.podia.com/free-author-journey-roadmap
(Get FREE Instant Access)

It is also recommended that you use the companion workbook, *Author Journey Success Workbook – Track Your Writing, Self-Publishing and Book Marketing From Start to Finish*, in order to follow along as you complete the exercises for each step in this book. I recommend it for tracking all your progress. It will help you officially start your journey, record your start date, set goals, write ideas and doodle designs as your move along your journey.

To get the paperback workbook via Amazon, visit: geni.us/authorworkbook

All books are also available for online purchase on other websites such as barnesandnoble.com, and lots of other retailer websites.

Psssst...want the workbook for free as a downloadable editable file? It's included in my companion Author Journey Roadmap Workshop Training Bundle! The package contains a recorded workshop training video where I present and discuss the 7 steps contained in this book, special author guests, a Q&A session, an electronic version of my Author Journey Workbook, Author Tips and Advice, plus an extra gift: Defining Your Ideal Audience.

Visit this link to learn more about the companion training:

https://geni.us/author-workshop

1

Foundation and Goals

Step 1: Foundation and Goals

Establish a Strong Foundation

No matter what type of book you are writing, whether it is a short story, non-fiction self-help book, children's book, memoir, mystery/suspense thriller, or a historical fiction novel, it's important to start with a strong foundation, as well as a clear vision. This includes writing a premise for your book.

A premise for a book is like a foundation for a house. What is a foundation? Is it a concrete slab? For a physical building, yes; but for a book, it starts with an idea, which turns into a vision with a strong purpose. All foundations have several things in common – they should be strong, well designed and built to last. It's also important to set realistic goals to help you design, construct, write, publish and market your book. ***Refer to the My Foundation section in the companion workbook for the exercises and worksheets for this chapter.***

Exercise 1a. Establish Your Foundation

Begin by answering the following questions. Use the companion workbook (p. 7) or write your answers on a blank piece of paper, journal, or on your computer.

   a. ***What is the premise for your book?*** *If you are writing fiction, include your main character, the goal of the main character and what situation he/she is facing; if you are writing non-fiction, include a statement of the book's basic concept and purpose.*
   b. ***Why are you writing this book?*** *List 3 reasons why you love to write.*
   c. ***Who is your audience?*** *Define your audience (age, gender, interests, etc.)*
   d. ***Why would someone enjoy or benefit from your book?*** *Will your book entertain or evoke emotion (fiction), or will your book help the world in some way and solve a problem (non-fiction)?*
   e. ***Can your book be turned into a series?*** *If so, how will your book series be interconnected?*

Create a vision.

You also need a strong vision for your book and your ultimate goal. Close your eyes and envision you book. What does your book look like?

Exercise 1b. Envision Your Book

The purpose of this exercise is to first envision the answers to questions in your head.

    a. *Can you see your book?*
    b. *What does it look like?*
    c. *How does it feel?*
    d. *Is it a thick, heavy book, or a thin lightweight book?*
    e. *Is your book square or rectangular?*
    f. *How many books do you see? Do you see one book, or a book series?*
    g. *Is your book an electronic book, a paperback, or a hard cover book? Is it all three? Is your book suitable for an audio book?*
    h. *Draw one or more versions of your front cover. Remember it's only a draft but will spark many ideas!*

Exercise 1c. Doodle Your Book Cover

For this next exercise, picture a 3-dimensional rectangle or square. In fact, take out your favorite journal right now and draw a rectangle or square shape to represent your book cover. Picture your book title on the front cover, along with your name as the author. Now write a few words on the cover. If you're not sure what the title of your book will be yet, write the words "My Book" on the front of the book. Take a few minutes and doodle ideas for your title and cover. **If you are using the companion workbook (which I hope you are), use the 3-dimensional book cover images to jot notes and doodle your book cover ideas.**

Start Your Journey

Decide right now when you will start your writing journey. Mark the date on your calendar. Even if you have been secretly writing for years, pick a date when you will officially start your *new* journey. This will give you a fresh start. **If you are using the companion workbook, refer to Exercise 1d., "Make a Promise" to record your date to officially start your journey.**

At the beginning of my writing journey, I had several writing journals on-hand, but I felt like something was missing. I needed a special place for my wishes and dreams. I needed a place to write my heart's desires. One day, while browsing in a store, I saw it. It was beautiful: a spiral, hard-bound journal with a floral design on the front and back. It was a nice, large size of 8 ½ X 11, and the paper was crisp and lined. When I opened the journal, the first page was a thicker white page with capital gold letters which read "HAVE A GREAT DAY". It also included a double-sided page with sturdy plastic pockets to hold papers and notes. I loved it! It was perfect. So, I decided to treat myself to my "special" journal. It is from the Cynthia Rowley collection. I use it for ideas, notes, and special doodles of all my heart's desires with regards to writing.

When I found this amazing, visual appealing journal, I wasn't looking for it that day -- I accidentally stumbled upon it as I was browsing. Sometimes the best things happen when you are least expecting it.

I would recommend that you treat yourself to a "special" notebook where you can jot down fresh ideas or use it for writing and doodling anytime you feel like it. When I say doodling, I mean draw your book cover, doodle your story's characters, and write book title ideas in fancy lettering. Writing and doodling ideas truly helps things in your imagination come to life. I do most of my writing on my laptop, but my special journal is where I jot down my ideas initially. I like to think of it as my secret idea book.

If you prefer to work electronically, you can use your favorite app to write down your ideas. Another idea is an electronic tablet. A few years back, my husband surprised me with an electronic writing and drawing tablet called the reMarkable (with a capital "M" as the 3rd letter) tablet. I love it for writing ideas, and drawing. I used it to draw some illustrations for my coloring and activity books. The reMarkable tablet also changed my life because it opened me up to a whole new world of drawing.

During my writing, publishing and marketing journey, there was so much information I was taking in, reading, learning and trying to keep track of, so I started writing it all down, as a daily log. I found that it was the only way for me to keep track of every little thing I did, and I knew that I would need to refer back to my notes at some point. I used Microsoft Word to log my notes so that I could take advantage of the search feature later, to look up something I did months prior. Microsoft Word is also the app that I use to write and format my books.

In addition to my special Cynthia Rowley journal notebook for writing down ideas and notes, I also kept different types of journals and notebooks in different rooms in the house for when ideas popped into my head, which would happen frequently. I found that the more I wrote, the freer and more creative I felt.

You have now reached the midpoint of the first step in your author journey, so you deserve a break!

Take a 5-minute break now and do the following:

1. *Sit in a comfortable chair.*
2. *Close your eyes if desired.*
3. *Take several deep breaths.*
4. *Open your heart and mind to new possibilities.*

When you open yourself up to new ideas, you are one step closer to achieving your heart's desire.

If you are excited about writing, the ideas will come naturally. Ideas would pop into my head in the morning, in the evening, and sometimes in the middle of the night. I had so many ideas about books I wanted to write, that I felt overwhelmed at times. I even kept a small notebook on my nightstand next to my bed. Be sure to keep a notebook handy at home or when you are on the go to jot down those important book ideas!

Compare your book with a blueprint for a beautiful house or building.

- Imagine that the front of a house is your book cover. Although your book cover has not been designed yet, it still helps to have a mental image of your book.
- The door is your first page and will be what readers will first see when they enter the building.
- Different floors of a building are the chapters of your book.
- If your book is non-fiction, then imagine that you are the main character and the owner of the building, and the rest of the people in the building include everyone who contributed to the building of your book. If your book is fictional, the people who work in the building are the characters in your book.
- The people who visit the building are the readers of your book.
- The groundskeeper, gardener, landscaper, and maintenance crew are the team of followers you build who help you take care of your building.

Even before a structure is built, pieces of the building may already be created. This may include doors, steps and furniture, or even the cinder blocks that create the walls. The reason I am mentioning this is because the same may be true with your book – you may already have sections of your book, pages, even chapters, written already. You may have some stories tucked away that you wrote years ago, but you're not sure where to begin, or how to put it all together to make a book. You might have ideas for a book, and notes you jotted down in journals, on your computer, or on electronic tablets. You might also have sketched pictures of characters or images you envision on your book cover. No matter where the pieces of your book may be, they do exist. And I'm here to tell you that they can in fact be turned into a book. I had mounds of content, both in my head, on paper, and on my computer.

I know what you're thinking – that this is hard work, and you just want to publish your book already. You might be thinking, *"Get on with it!"* I'm here to say, *"I hear ya!"* And I can tell you that with a little elbow grease, determination and dedication, it will happen for sure – and I will help you get there.

The reason I wrote this book is to share my experiences with you and walk you through the process. The fact that you bought this book and started reading it means you are serious, and you are on your way to being a published author.

You have already decided that you will write and self-publish a book, so from this point forward, it's full steam ahead. So, roll up your sleeves and let the journey begin!

Repeat after me: *"I am on my way to becoming an author. I can do this!"*

Now repeat it every day, at least 3 times a day. Write it down on an index card and put it somewhere you will see it each and every day. You can write your own version of the statement. Put it in your wallet, tape it to your medicine cabinet, or put it on the dashboard in your car. Have faith in yourself and in the universe. Believe.

"Know what you want and continue to want it. You will get it if you combine desire and faith.

The power of desire when combined with faith becomes invincible."

~Christian D. Larson

My Journey Thoughts

Why do I write? I just didn't wake up one morning and decide to write. I've always loved to write, but I also loved to do a lot of other things too – I always loved to draw, create things, fix things, tell jokes, listen to music, cook, dance, and the list goes on and on. Sometimes it's hard to know exactly what you should do in your life. So, while I was trying to figure out what to do in life, I saved things. I saved stories I wrote and pictures I drew as a child. I saved all the watercolors and acrylic paintings I created in high school. I wrote in a journal for years and then threw out things I wrote for fear or shame that no one would care that I wrote it. When I was a young girl, I watched reruns of the series called "The Walton's" and envied the oldest child named John-Boy, played by actor Richard Thomas. John-Boy wrote secretly and hid the pages of his book under his mattress. I did the same thing.

When I was in college, I was told I had to pick a major area of study. I had no idea what I wanted to specialize in. At first, I picked something that I was *least* interested in: Accounting. I'm not sure if I picked Accounting because it was at the top of the list, or because the college counselor suggested that I pick something related to business. Nevertheless, there was a silver lining. Majoring in Accounting meant you had to be in the school of business, and one required class was Fortran programming. I learned programming and flowcharting and became fascinated with computers. So, I decided that computers would be my career. I always loved computers, and I still do, but the writing thing was always there. Flash forward 20 years – as an Instructional Designer and eLearning Developer, I write educational content and design and develop online learning, but again, the author in me was always there. So, I found a way to get back to my dream of writing. Over 10 years ago, in my spare time, I started writing online articles, and then short stories. I had 2 short stories published in a real book and then I was hooked. As I continued to work in the IT Training and Design industry, I started pursuing my dream of writing and self-publishing.

So, what do we do when we discover we enjoy something? We all have things we love to do, and sometimes we find ways to incorporate it into daily life. Maybe you love to cook and secretly wish you could have your own cooking show with a bestselling cookbook, but instead life got in the way, so you cook for your family and stop there. Maybe you love science fiction or mystery suspense, and you have pages and pages of short mysteries you have written, and you secretly wish you could write a mystery or science-fiction series; but instead, you read thrillers and mystery books and watch detective shows on TV and keep saying "I could have written that!". Maybe you doodle all the time and absolutely love to draw – and every time you go to a bookstore, you imagine a children's picture book that you wrote and illustrated.

It's ok to dream, and it's ok to imagine. It's also more than ok to chase your dreams and achieve them. Isn't that the point of life?

What is the underlying basis or reason for your story?

Think about the reason you are writing your book. Whatever your book is about, it's important to believe in your story, and make it the best possible book in your genre.

Are you excited about your story? Being happy and excited about your story is equally important and will resonate in your writing. Do you feel grateful, emotional, scared, nervous, or feeling other feelings? Imagine how you will feel when you are holding your first book in your hand. Take a minute to identify your feelings. ***See Exercise 1e. Identify Your Feelings in the companion workbook.***

Do you have a multitude of ideas and stories, but don't know which one is best for your first book?

Maybe you just want to write, but you don't know which idea is best. You cringe at the thought of going to a writing critique group for fear that someone will criticize your ideas. You won't know unless you try. For now, I want you to think about the reason you are writing a book. It's important to write for the right reason.

Idea Validation – Should You Write From the Heart or Write to Market?

Should you write a novel, short reads or a non-fiction self-help book? Should you write from the heart or write to market? The choice will ultimately be yours. However, there are a few things to consider before making your decision.

There are plenty of people who will tell you to write to market. There are even books written on why and how to write to market. Should you write to market? Yes and no. How about a combination of the two? Let me explain. If you write purely for market, that means you are picking a topic only because it's trending and popular. Writing to market about a topic you know nothing about can be a disappointment and can get you into trouble. If you write to market, your heart may not be into it, which may show through in your writing. If you write to market purely to make a profit, you will be writing for the wrong reason. If you decide to write a nonfiction book on a hot topic that Johnny Entrepreneur told you to write about, you also have to research the topic and make sure you know what you are talking about. So before writing about Robotics in the 21st Century because someone tells you it's the hottest topic and guaranteed to be a bestseller, think twice. If your heart is set on writing a nonfiction book to help the world, why not consider writing about a topic that you know a lot about?

Writing should be something you enjoy, not something you dread. Dreading is exactly what you will be feeling if you pick a topic that you know nothing about, and care nothing about. If you enjoy fishing and love to travel, chances are that you probably know a lot more than you think on the topic. With a little research, you can discover what type of travel books are trending, then harness that interest into a bestselling book. This strategy of using your own idea but keeping trends in mind offers you the best of both worlds: a topic you enjoy writing about but with a trending twist. The possibilities are endless!

If you are interested in writing a novel, and it's your heart's desire, that is what you should write. However, if you have never written a single fictional story before, consider writing a few short stories first to test the waters. Who is your main character? Who is the antagonist and the protagonist? Did you define your plot? How will your novel be different than the thousands if not millions of novels out there?

What Should You Write?

No matter what you write about, practice makes perfect. Just remember – you don't have to write a novel first if it doesn't feel right. About 10 years ago, when I started getting serious about writing, my original plan was to plunge into deep waters and write a novel right off the bat. Heck, I can't even swim! Something didn't feel right. I quickly realized I had to pull the reins a bit and learn more about the entire author process, including publishing and marketing. I also had to determine if writing a novel would in fact be a *novel* idea. Would it be marketable? Would my audience trust me? In my case, I had been writing technical books, like training manuals for years. I had started writing short stories, but was I ready to write a novel? Did I have the time to write a novel? How would I get the word out? Should I pitch the idea to an agent or look into self-publishing? How long would this take? A thousand questions popped into my head.

First, I decided to do a little self-reflection and research. I made a list of all the topics I wanted to write about, and then I circled the topics for which I already had content. I also considered my schedule and my availability. This is definitely something you want to consider. Do you have the type of day job that will allow you to spend a few hours each night, or each week to devote to your writing? Will your family understand if you lock yourself in the den several nights a week while you type away on your computer? Writing a book is a commitment. It all depends on what you are ready for, and what you have time for. It's also a matter of trial and error. Remember that Rome wasn't built in a day.

In my case, I decided to start small but think big. I not only had to decide which topic to write about first and if it would be marketable, but I also had to decide if I wanted to pursue traditional publishing vs. self-publishing. At the time, I started hearing more and more about how self-publishing helps you get your books on Amazon much faster than traditional publishing. So, I decided to give it a try as my first writing experiment. I embarked on a self-publishing course to learn the ins and outs of self-publishing. *I discuss more about publishing options and why I selected self-publishing later in this book in Step 6.*

As I mentioned, when I first got serious about writing, I had this idea in my head that I would write a historical fiction novel. I even named all my characters and wrote a few chapters. Then I realized that there was something more important I had to do first: build my brand. If you write a fantastic book and it's published and online, it's very exciting; but *remember* if you are an unknown author, and if the genre you are writing in is too saturated, your book will get lost in the sea of millions of other books.

If you are dreaming of writing a 300-page science fiction novel but you feel overwhelmed, consider writing some shorter sci-fi stories, or maybe even a series. If you are torn between writing non-fiction and fiction, don't feel like you have to settle on just one. There are plenty of authors who write both fiction and non-fiction. One example is Joanna Penn. She writes non-fiction books to help authors, and she also writes bestselling thrillers and dark fantasy novels. It's more acceptable nowadays to be an author who writes in different genres and self-publishes their own books.

So, whether you decide to write in one genre or multiple genres, the important thing is to build your brand first, get your audience to know you. Help your audience see what you can offer them. How can you help them? Can you entertain them by writing a romance mystery novel? Can you solve a problem by writing a nonfiction book? You will keep hearing me say this, but again, the possibilities are endless.

Keeping my schedule in mind and how this was my first experiment with writing and self-publishing, I decided to start with something I felt comfortable writing about, and something I knew I could market.

For my first book, I decided to write a series of computer-themed lessons, leveraging the content that I already had on-hand. I had been collecting computer tips and tricks for a wide variety of software applications which I taught over the years, especially in Microsoft Office. I made the decision to start with non-fiction rather than fiction for several reasons:

- I had limited time for writing.
- There was already content on hand that I could leverage for my books.
- My nonfiction books would solve a problem.
- The topic was popular and would be easier to market than a novel by an unknown author.
- Writing and marketing books related to my career would help me build my brand.

As I started outlining and planning content for my first book, I started thinking about the possibility of having a series of books. A book series is an option you may want to consider ahead of time, so you can plan your series accordingly. This can be fiction or non-fiction. There are many benefits of having a book series. If readers are interested in the first book in your series, they may be interested in other books in your series. Depending on your genre, if your books are fiction such as mystery/suspense, you could include a cliffhanger at the end of each book which will entice readers to purchase the next book. If you setup a book series on Kindle Direct Publishing, you can create a series page on Amazon to promote all the books in your series on one page.

Define Measurable Goals

Next, let's forge ahead and move into goal setting. What is your goal? Is it to write one book, or a book series? Do you want to write a book this month or this year? If your answer is that you want to write a book this month, it's probably not a reasonable goal, especially if you are working full-time. I'm not saying it's impossible. All things are possible, depending on how much time and effort you put into it. There are online writing challenges like Novel Writing Month (or NaNoWriMo) where the goal is to write 50,000 words in 30 days, but this does require a big commitment. I considered using the NaNoWriMo but quickly realized it was not for me. When I started getting serious about writing, my plate was already full, and since there are only so many hours in a day, I knew the goal of 50,000 words in 30 days was not realistic for my schedule. If you can devote several hours per day to writing, including weekends, the NaNoWriMo may be attainable. I was only able to devote 1-2 hours, several evenings (not including weekends), so I decided that I wanted to write at my own pace.

In summary, I recommend that you start small and then add as you go. If you set your goal too high, you may get frustrated that you are not meeting your goal. Instead, take baby steps and consider setting a small goal of writing for 15 minutes a day. If you love writing, 15 minutes will pass quickly and you may find yourself writing for 30 minutes, or even an hour. When that happens, you can celebrate because you will be exceeding your goal.

Exercise 1f: Goals

What is your writing goal? When can you complete your first, second, and third drafts of your manuscript? You can break it down chapter by chapter to make it easier. Take a few moments and write down the answers. Be sure to include realistic, attainable dates and times when defining your writing goals.

Refer to the "Define Measurable Goals" section in the companion workbook, to record the goals for your writing journey. Once you have finished this exercise, continue with the next section below.

Find Your Inner Strength

Now that you have defined your writing goals, are you ready to climb up the steps of success to complete your book? In the event that any barriers, distractions, or interruptions occur, what will you do to move forward? The answer is simple but sometimes left unnoticed. You have a special power which can help you forge ahead: inner strength. We all have inner strength, and sometimes it's just a matter of recognizing it and harnessing it to reach your goals.

Think of three things in your life that you have accomplished. These can be little things or big things. It can be when you learned how to ride a bike, when you cooked your first meal by yourself, or when you went on your first job interview. Whatever these things may be, it took courage for you to do what you did. Now it's time to identify and channel your strength and forge ahead with your writing. You can do it!

Remind yourself everyday that you have inner strength. If someone or something gets you down, imagine that you are climbing a hill and a force pulls you up. You are a strong person, and you can accomplish anything. Remember that each and every day as you move forward along your author journey.

Refer to Exercise 1g. in the companion workbook for a special exercise on inner strength.

Be a Visionary – Create a Vision Board

Are you a visionary? A visionary is someone who thinks about and plans the future with imagination and wisdom. Earlier in this chapter, you created a vision of your book. Now that you have imagined what your book might look like and set the date of when you will start creating your book, it's time to go a step further by creating a vision board.

Exercise 1h. Create a Vision Board

Your vision board should represent your vision for the future. It can contain as many thoughts, messages, quotes, images and pictures as you want, and you can change them or add to them as often as you like. I like to use a cork board bulletin board for my vision board. You can also use a thick poster board for a vision board as well. It can also be an electronic board if you prefer. You can use tools like Canva to create an electronic vision board or use Microsoft PowerPoint.

For your author journey, you can add a note on your vision board about something you want to accomplish tomorrow, next week, or next year. As time passes, you may find yourself removing images and tacking up new ones. For each of my books, while I was working on them, I would put placeholders for each one, including a title draft. If I didn't know what my book titles would be, I would call them Book 1, Book 2, and Book 3. I like to work in 3's for each of my book series. Once the front covers were finished, I printed out small color versions of each books and taped them to my vision board, along with launch dates. I also like to print quotes and tape them to my vision board. You can put whatever you like on your vision board, but for the purpose of your author journey, be sure to include a symbol for your book and author dreams and visions. This may include a trophy, bestseller banner, increased sales bar chart, and inspirational quotes for motivation.

Here is an example of what a vision board may look like:

Refer to the Create a Vision Board exercise in the companion workbook for additional instructions on how to create your vision board.

Select Your Genre or Topic

By now, you may already know exactly what your book will be about. However, if you're not sure what genre is best, or you are having a difficult time deciding on a genre, ask yourself these questions:

Are you interested in creating:

- ➢ Non-fiction? What problem will your book solve?
- ➢ Fictional short stories or a novel? Consider a novella or short read as a starting point.
- ➢ Children's book? Do you have a creative poem or fun story tucked away that a child might like?
- ➢ Zero-content books? Consider creating these for fun, or as companions to your main book. Zero-content books or near-zero content books include journals, notebooks, diaries, puzzle books, workbooks, logbooks, sheet music pages, etc.

Go to Amazon.com and browse in different book categories for ideas. Consider a genre that makes the most sense for you to write about, and not just what is trending. Look at the bestselling books and categories. While you are there, take note of some of the book covers and titles which catch your eye. Take some screen shots to look at later to help you decide.

*Need more help deciding? Get your copy of **The Writing and Brainstorming Book: 10 Ideas to Crafting Bestsellers**. For more information, visit my bookshelf:* ameliaswritingcorner.com/amelias-books *or send me a message via this link:* https://geni.us/askamelia *and I'll send you information on how to get the book!*

Congratulations!

You have now reached the 1st milestone in your journey!

2

The Writing Process

Step 2: The Writing Process

Do What You Love

Now that you have laid the foundation for your book, it's time to move ahead and write you book. Do you love to write? I hope the answer is a big YES! If you are like me, you love to write day and night. If you love to write, then this step will be an easier one to climb, and I don't have to convince you to get that notebook out or go open up your laptop – and start writing. Instead, it will be something that happens effortlessly and something you enjoy. In this case, skip down to the **Let's Begin** section below.

What If You Don't Love to Write

If you don't love the writing process, but you have a story to tell, then it might be best to find someone to work with who can help you get the words down on paper. One idea is to have someone interview you and record the interview. The interview should be very detailed and filled with lots of questions so you can not only explain the story of what you want to write about, but be able to tell the whole story, bit by bit, until it is transcribed and transformed into a book. Either way, whether you love to write or only like to tell stories, and now want to turn it into a book, it's time to move on to the next section below. It's time to begin.

Let's Begin

If you're not sure where to start, this section will help you prepare for the writing process.

If you're following along using the companion workbook, refer to the Track Your Writing Progress section, which includes exercises and prompts for writing an outline, establishing a writing schedule and setting target dates.

Instead of telling you to just start writing, there are several things that I like to do when I write, and I'm going to recommend that you do these as well:

1. **Start with an Outline** – This can be as simple as a list in Notepad, Microsoft Word, or any other app. If you prefer, write your outline in a notebook. Create your outline now! *Refer to in the Track Your Writing Progress section in the companion workbook for an outline example.*

2. **Building a Strong Writing Habit** – Add a daily reminder in your phone for when you will write. Whether it's 15 minutes or an hour, the reminder will keep you on point.

3. **Discipline Yourself** – Be sure to discipline yourself. Oh, did I mention the word discipline? Yes, it is intentional that I just repeated the word *discipline* three times. I was brought up in a strict environment with lots of rules, and I attended Catholic school. Therefore, I learned discipline at a young age. I understand that your situation may be different. The way I learned discipline was to follow instructions. If you are ever too tired or find yourself procrastinating, try giving yourself an instruction – remind yourself to write, and remember how important it is to write. To achieve your goal of writing each day will require a few things: the belief that you can do it (and trust me, you can!), commitment, support from others, and organization. Breathe a happy sigh of relief each day, and give yourself a pat on the back for each word you write.

4. **Your Writing Schedule** – Using the suggestions I mentioned earlier in this chapter, once you have setup your writing environment and you are committed to writing, it is key that you stick to your schedule as often as possible. If you love writing, this will not be a burden for you. Instead, it will be a welcoming break in your hectic day. If you miss a day, don't fret. You can always add an extra 30 minutes the next day. Remember, you are in control. *Refer to the companion workbook to record and track your writing schedule, and for a Writing and Tracking Schedule Log.* Here's an example of my writing schedule while working full-time.
    *   For each of my nine books, on average, I allotted 1-2 hours, at least 3 evenings a week for a period of three months for writing. At times, I was able to work a flexible schedule, which meant I had off every other Friday. I looked forward to any time off to devote to my writing. For my technology series, I also used a portion of that time to record,

edit and publish companion training videos. For my children's rhyming books, since the stories were short, more of the time was spent working with my illustrator and page layouts. For my children's coloring and activity books, this was a different kind of series, which required a lot more time for laying out educational activities, working with coloring pages and organizing the pages and illustrations.

- On weekends, I usually never wrote on Saturdays, which was always packed with errands, family time, and fun events. On Sundays, unless there were family events, I devoted anywhere from 2 to 4 hours of writing in the afternoon or evening.

5. **Set Writing Target Dates** – In conjunction with your writing schedule, schedule several target dates for your first, second and third drafts. *You can find a writing target worksheet in the in the companion workbook.*

6. **Write First, Edit Later** - If you are writing from your heart, the words will flow like water from a faucet. Don't stop and edit while you write, which can interfere with the creative process. Just keep writing and then return later to edit.

7. **Last Minute Things to Do**:
- If you're having problems focusing, or getting started, clean your desk and/or organize your office – it's therapeutic, and will help you have the right mindset to start a new chapter.
- If you feel frustrated, burnt out or tired, it's important to take a rest and relaxation break. Do something fun and take care of you! Take a hot bath, take a 10-minute catnap, or treat yourself to a healthy snack.
- If you feel tired and stiff, it's time for a 5-minute stretch break. Stand up and do 5 arm circles, 5 neck rolls, and a few deep breaths. Exhale slowly. Drink a glass a water and remember to stay hydrated. Feeling sleepy? I like to keep a bottle of peppermint essential oils on my desk, because a quick whiff of peppermint scented oil or even peppermint tea can keep you alert and give you a boost of energy.

Writing Tools and Methods

For all my writing, editing and book layouts, I use Microsoft Word. Other tools I use include Snagit, Canva, and Adobe Photoshop Elements, but these are primarily used for image editing. There are many other Word Processing programs and other tools used by authors like Scrivener, InDesign and other software programs. I purchased Scrivener while I started writing my first book, but I decided to hold off on using Scrivener for several reasons:

- My first book was a how-to book focusing on tips, tricks and shortcuts on Microsoft Word, so I decided to stick to using software that I knew inside out. Also, I felt comfortable applying all the bells and whistles of a book using Word, including a table of contents, page numbering and heavy-duty formatting.
- Scrivener seemed to be a great tool for chapter books, where you need help organizing your content, so I decided to return to it at a later time.

In regard to what software to use when writing, I would say it's best to stick with something you know. If you need help with the formatting, that's covered in *Step 5. The Formatting and Editing Process*.

The Method I Used For This Book

The book you are currently reading, like many nonfiction books, was not written at one sitting, in sequential chapters. It took several months of organizing over 200 pages of notes, content, and ideas that I logged over a 4 to 5-year period of time. My other books took an average of 3 months to write. So why did it take me a period of 5 years to organize and write this book? That is how long it took me to learn and practice the process of writing, editing, publishing, and marketing. I did this part-time while working full-time. Every situation will be different. The more your write, the more confident you will feel about your writing. Just remember that practice makes perfect.

Write everything down.

As I mentioned previously, when I embarked on the writing and self-publishing process, I knew there was going to be an enormous amount of information I had to remember, practice, and refer to. So, I decided to log what I did each and every day so I could keep track of everything. I logged what I was doing, what I learned, what worked, what didn't work, links to refer to, and screen shots of steps I took to get things done. The main place I logged everything was in a Microsoft Word document. I am a stickler for making backups of files, so I backed up my file every day and also made extra backup copies on an external drive. In case I forget to mention it later, for whatever you write, back it up! It's better to have 10 copies of your first draft vs. no backups at all if your computer decides to have a conniption.

Celebrate each and every day.

Some days I was too busy or tired to work on anything in the evening, but I didn't let that get me down. If I set a goal for myself to write 30 minutes and I ended up writing for 15 minutes, I still considered that an accomplishment. So, remember to celebrate each and every day, for all you do, including balancing life, work, exercising, family, fun, and most important, writing!

Get organized.

Once you have the outline of your book drafted, it's time to begin the writing process. If you are writing a non-fiction book, it may mean leveraging notes from another document, or transcribing handwritten notes for a journal or logbook. I literally reviewed over 200 pages of my electronic notes, page by page, and then incorporated the content into my new document, for this book. As I leveraged content that I journaled previously, I wrote paragraphs and more paragraphs to make sense out of it. Some days I would be on a roll with a particular chapter or section, and other days, the words would not flow out so easily.

Thinking back to when I wrote short stories, once the characters and premise were defined, I usually wrote the story at one sitting, and then I went back to edit it over a series of evenings. This was flash fiction, with a word count of under 1000 words, thus the reason I was able to write it in a short period of time.

If you are writing fiction, such as a novel, you can break it up in chapters. So, perhaps you can write one chapter per week or per month. How you write and when you write may vary depending on your writing style and what makes sense for you. It will also depend on the type of fictional story and the length. If you want to write a novel but need to practice, you can start with short stories.

If your heart's desire is to write a novel, here are some guidelines to get started:

- Storyline and Plot – Write a short description of what the novel will be about.

- Characters – Make a list of all the characters, including their names, and indicate who is the protagonist and who is the antagonist.
- Family/Character Tree – To further define the relationships of all the characters and, consider sketching a family tree including ages, professions, relation to one another, and any other pertinent details which may add to the story.
- Chapter Planning – Think about and describe the chapters for your book.
- Write Your First Draft – Write from the heart, whether that be a page, a chapter, or more. Remember write first, edit later.

If you are planning on writing a nonfiction book, here are some guidelines to get started:

- Purpose of the book – Write a short description of what the book will be about and what problem it will solve.
- Chapter Planning – Make a list of the topics you will write about in each chapter. Now might be a good time to go back to your outline and create subheadings for each section or chapter.
- Start Researching – When writing nonfiction, remember to not only include examples that your audience can relate to, but to check all facts and information. Now is a good time to start researching your topic and making a list of any references to include in the back of your book.

Create a Writing Oasis

What is a writing oasis? This is a special area, spot, room, or location where you are planning to write. It's important to have a quiet place to write and work. Ideally, a separate room or office is best. Do not work on your kitchen table for several reasons: it's not ergonomic, and it's the busiest room in the house; and let's not forget about the temptation to eat something while you work, which will cause more distractions. You can have more than one writing location, but there should be one main location where you can go hide and write. If you don't have an office in your house, maybe there is a comfy chair you love to sit in and write. If you do have an office or den with a writing desk, clean your desk! Clutter is no good when writing, at least for me it isn't. I'm not saying my desk is immaculate, but it's organized in such a way that I feel like I can open my laptop and get started right away. You don't want to have to move stuff to the side of your kitchen table each time you want to write. Ideally, you want to have one or more spots you can go to when you get a writing urge.

Electronic vs. Handwriting – What's Better?

I do both. I write most of my content on my laptop and then I back it up religiously. But the buck doesn't stop there. I have um-teen journals and notebooks that I mostly keep in my office that I also use to write down brainstorming ideas or sketch pictures and diagrams that pop-up in my head at odd times of the day and night. I keep at least one small journal book at bedside, and sometimes I carry a small one in my purse when I leave the house. Why? Because if you love writing, once you start writing, all kinds of ideas pop in your head at different times of the day. When they do, you'll want to write them down right away. Just jot it down quickly, and then you can elaborate on it later. The point is to harness each idea that emerges as soon as you think of it – you never know which one might turn into a bestselling book idea.

Writing in the Middle of the Night?

So, it's 2am and suddenly you find yourself awake in the middle of the night. It's not your partner's snoring that is keeping you up – it's the brainstorm idea that just popped in your head. The realistic part of you tells you to try to go back to sleep and write it down in the morning – but the creative, fun-loving, authorpreneur part of you is too excited to sleep – you know you must write this down now before it flies right out of your head.

This has happened to me plenty of times. Sometimes I grab my iPhone and type my ideas in the Notes app. Other times I would turn on a flashlight app on my iPhone, grab my handy bedside journal and write down what I was thinking. But one night, that wasn't going to cut it. I needed to sit up with the light on and pour out a chapter immediately. So, I took my medium-sized journal, which has more room to write in vs. my mini-journal, into the bathroom, sat on the edge of the tub and wrote away. I could not stop writing that night. I wrote for about an hour. And then I breathed a sigh of relief, noticed it was after 3am, and decided I better try to get a couple more hours of sleep before the daily grind of my full-time day job would begin. So, I moseyed on back to bed, fumbling around in the dark. I forgot to let my eyes adjust from the bright light to the darkness, so as I climbed back into bed, laying my journal and pen down on my nightstand, I stacked it on top of my iPhone, night mask and box of tissues, causing a slight but noisy avalanche of stuff crashing to the ground. My iPhone flashlight app came in handy at that point as I picked everything up and then went to sleep. In the morning, hubby asked what all the racket was in the middle of the night. LOL

Reduce Distractions, Noise and Stress and Increase Writing Time

Although it is impossible to eliminate noise and create a peaceful calm environment, here are some things you can do to reduce distractions and noise so you can better concentrate on your writing:

Don't watch live TV – Instead of watching live TV, set your DVR to record your favorite shows. I hardly ever watch live TV. Watching live TV means you must sit and wait while commercials play. If you record a movie to watch, you can save time by fast-forwarding through commercials. So instead of spending 2 hours watching a movie, you may only need 90 minutes or less. There's 30 minutes of writing time!

Find a Job with Flexible Hours – If you are working Monday through Friday, all day, why not consider a 4-day work week? You can also consider other work schedules like working 9 days and having the 10th day off. This is exactly the type of schedule I worked a few years ago when I needed more time to work on my books. Many companies are allowing employees to work flexible hours. It doesn't hurt to ask. If your current company doesn't allow any flexibility and is working you to the bone, then it may be time to evaluate your job situation. If writing is something you want to do, you may have to research options to consider a more flexible work schedule.

Cook in Batches – Deciding what to cook for dinner can not only be distracting, but it can also be downright time consuming. Is there a larger dinner you can cook one night so that's there's leftovers another night which will save you on cooking time? If you are cooking every single night, or even several nights, are there some nights that you can eat a quicker meal? A quicker meal might be eating breakfast for dinner. Consider freezing a few dinners for easy dinner nights as well. This can also be a time saver for breakfast. For example, I like to buy a bunch of avocados and when they are ripe, I cut and mash them, and then freeze them in small silicone containers. They are easy to thaw anytime for any meal.

Prepare at Night for an Easier Morning – If some evenings are just too busy and hectic for writing, is there ½ hour in the morning you can spare for writing, possibly before anyone else gets up? Maybe that means showering at night and laying your clothes out the night before. If you can do some light preparation every evening, the mornings can be easier and less stressful, and may allow for more writing time.

Motivational Quotes

As you continue along your writing journey, keep these quotes in mind, especially if you need help moving forward:

"You don't have to be great to start, but you have to start to be great."

~Zig Ziglar

"We do not need magic to change the world, we carry all the power we need inside ourselves already. We have the power to imagine better."

~ J.K. Rowling

"You must have a place to which you can go in your heart, your mind, or your home, almost every day, where you do not owe anyone and where no one owes you – a place that simply allows for the blossoming of something new and promising."

~ Joseph Campbell

Final Thoughts When Writing

Remember the analogy earlier about the house, when I asked you to envision the front of your book? Now, think about that same house or other structure being built. Imagine that the concrete has been poured and the foundation is completed. Next, the frame of the house is being constructed. The house is beginning to take shape, and so is your book!

Continue writing and keep writing until all chapters are complete. Remember, write first, then edit.

"Courage is the power to let go of the familiar."

~Raymond Lindquist

Congratulations!

You have now reached the 2nd milestone in your journey!

3

Learning, Doing Your Homework and Pre-Marketing

Step 3: Learning, Doing Your Homework and Pre-Marketing

So, you started writing a book and your draft is just about done. You start wondering what if anything you will do with your manuscript once it is completed. You dream of being a published author but have no idea where to begin. How does someone get their book on Amazon? Do you need a website? How do you let the world know about your book?

First and foremost, I want to explain how important it is to do your homework when it comes to getting your book published. I'll also list several ways you can begin to pre-market your book. Yes, that's what I said...pre-market. You might be thinking...but I don't even have a cover yet, let alone a following, so how could I possibly do pre-marketing? Not to worry, I'll explain.

Learning How to Be Successful – Turning Negativity into Positivity

How many people would you say you have come into contact with, throughout your whole life? You may or may not have thought about it much, but you have already met many pivotal people throughout your life who have impacted you in both a negative and positive way.

There are people all around you who influence you every day. Even if they are not sitting next to you, they are influencing you. These may be people in your family, your friends, your co-workers, your neighbors, people in the media, celebrities, people you meet on the street, in stores and restaurants, and everywhere.

Let's go back in the past for a moment. It all began when you were born, innocent and free. Once you came into contact with people, you were influenced in both a positive and negative way, and even in a neutral way.

As you grew, you learned from parents, teachers, other adults, and other children. You were impressionable at every age, and you are still impressionable.

Have you ever thought about why you love to write? Are you born with it, or is it a learned behavior? I tend to think that some of us are destined to write – maybe it's part of our genes, or maybe it's just a skillset we learn to love.

A Summarized Passage From My Journal:

When I was a little girl, I loved drawing, printing, and eventually cursive writing. When I was a teenager, I used to write in diaries and journals all the time. When I had my first crush, I wrote about it in a diary. When I was angry about something and found myself crying, I would write about it. I found writing to be therapeutic and a good outlet in a time when I felt stifled. You see, as a very young girl, I was restrained from things. I was brought up fairly strict and attended Catholic school. I was not like other kids who rode their bikes and went swimming. I did not learn how to ride a bike until I was a teenager, and I didn't even take swimming lessons until I was in my 20's. It's not that I wasn't happy – I was a fairly happy young girl. I did what I was told, didn't complain too much and appreciated what I had. We lived in a three story row house similar to the one seen on the movie "Moonstruck". Rules, school uniforms, strict regimes – it was just the way it was in Catholic school. I was taught to not speak until I was spoken to, which got me into trouble.

In second grade when I was only 7 years old, my teacher wrote something on my report card. The comment she wrote had a double meaning. On the report card, she wrote "Amelia likes to talk." When the report card was sent home, my father wasn't too happy. After all, a comment like that sounds like I was talking when I shouldn't have been talking. It could have also been taken as a compliment – perhaps what she was trying to say was that I liked to express myself, so maybe I was destined to be a speaker, or even a writer. I vaguely remember my father going to my school and meeting with my teacher. When he got home, he sat me down and told me what happened (there was some good news and some not-so-good news). The good news was that my teacher said I was a very good worker and finished my work quickly. The not so good news was that when I was finished, I would talk to and bother the other children. Yikes! I'm not sure why I was so chatty – maybe I was trying to help the other children instead of bothering them? Or maybe I was a chatter box because I was bored. Maybe I just wanted attention. No matter what the reason was, I remember initially feeling like I was scolded. Being brought up Catholic meant there were many rules to follow, and I always did what I was told and followed the rules. However, there's a flip side to every story, and in this case, there was a silver lining to be found. I recall telling another little girl that I got scolded by our teacher for talking, and how my father was called to the school. This must have resonated with me, as I remember telling the other little girl that I didn't think my teacher liked me. My teacher overheard and called me over and wanted to talk to me. Gulp! Her face is all but a faint memory but what she said is something I will remember always, as it had a very positive effect on my life. She reassured me and explained that it wasn't that she didn't like me – instead, it was just the opposite. She did indeed like me and enjoyed having me in her classroom. I still remember how I felt, standing there, awkward but relieved; embarrassed yet happy!

That day, I learned a valuable lesson: I learned that it was ok to be chatty, and it was ok to be me. I felt accepted, loved and supported. I still followed the rules at home and at school, but I was different after that day. I was more accepting and grateful.

So, when people ask me why I write or when I started writing, I usually tell them that I started writing as a little girl, for as long as I could remember. Pen and paper were destined to be in my hand. I write to get the words out that I may not be able to say. I write to feel better. I write because I can take my time and compose what I want to say, slowly and carefully. Words are a true form of expression. I write for the same reason a pianist loves to play the piano, and why a gymnast loves to do cartwheels. I write because I just love to write...'nuff said!

As you continue on your author journey, take notice of other successful people, including authors, teachers, coaches, and entrepreneurs. Look for a mentor. This person may be someone you meet by chance, or someone you never meet in person, but still learn a great deal from. Perhaps you already know this person. Maybe you met them as a child and always looked up to them. Maybe you met a teacher when you were in school who changed your life. The story about my second-grade teacher is just one small example of how someone can make a *huge* positive impact on your life by saying just one thing. Perhaps the most pivotal, positive person in your life is sitting next to you right now.

If there are unsupportive people in your life (and there will be), do not let it get you down. The important thing is to not feed into the negative energy and behavior. Most of us come into contact with positive and negative people every single day, whether in person or online. Remember it's not what happens to you, but how you react to a situation that matters.

If you want to be successful, you have to surround yourself with successful people. Even if it's not possible to be around other successful people all day and every day, you can begin small and surround yourself with success in other ways. You can watch inspirational videos, read articles written by successful people, or look at motivational pictures and images. I guarantee this will boost your confidence and help you achieve your writing goals.

Doing Your Homework

As children, it's just a given that you have to finish your homework in order to do well in school. As an adult, we sometimes have to create our own homework in order to get ahead and achieve success. To me, homework assignments are like items on a to do list, ranging from simple tasks to more complex assignments.

To be a successful writer and author is like any other profession: to excel in this business, you must do your research. This may include, and is not limited to following bestselling authors, educating yourself on how to run a business, learning how to market different types of books, researching book covers for your genre, and identifying what you can do now vs. later to ensure your books are successful.

If you're following along using the companion workbook, refer to the exercises in the Research and Pre-Marketing section.

Get Active Online

Have you started doing online research to see what other authors are up to? Start by following other authors and author groups and engage with them. Look at their books and download free samples. But – DON'T COPY from other authors – instead, LEARN from them. Here's how:

- Join author groups on Facebook, LinkedIn, or other social media.
- Post questions on author groups and get active to learn what works and what doesn't work for other authors.
- Engage online and post about your book to get advice.
- Don't limit yourself to just author groups; consider small business groups, local community groups, and so forth. Now is the time to join groups pertaining to the topic of your book. Remember to select groups which are a good fit for your genre. For example, if you are writing a children's book, follow and join teacher groups, library websites, and children's author groups. Next, engage, engage, and engage! Post about your upcoming book and ask lots of questions. Be a squeaky wheel and make your online rounds. Share what you have done so far, and offer to help others who are just starting out as well.

Refer to Exercise 3a. in the companion workbook for an exercise and worksheet on joining and connecting with Author Groups.

Attend Classes and Workshops

Are there any classes, local workshops or writing critique groups you can join? When I decided to embark on writing a children's series, I joined the Society of Children's Book Writers and Illustrators, which opened up a whole network of resources, workshops, and local events. I also joined a local writing critique group comprised of teachers, writers, and children's book enthusiasts to meet with and share my writing ideas. Each week, we would meet and read our children's stories to each other and critique each other's work. This turned out to be extremely helpful and was excellent for feedback!

Do Your Book Research

It's never too early to start doing research on books in your genre to help you plan on deciding on a book title, book cover, keywords, and book categories.

When you get to step 5 in this book which is *The Formatting and Editing Process*, you want to be prepared with some ideas about your book title and book cover. Start now by combing through books, either online or in local bookstores for ideas. If researching online, go to Amazon and check out the bestselling books in your genre. It's easy – just follow these steps:

1. From the Amazon home page, select Best Sellers on the upper left.
2. Next, click in the Any Department menu, select Books.
3. Overall Amazon Best Sellers will be displayed first. To narrow down by genre, select a genre under the Books menu. Imagine seeing your book listed in the top 100 or even the top 10 list!
4. Look at the top 10 or 20 books in your genre and take notice of the titles and book covers. Take notice if any books in the same genre have something in common. For fiction vs. nonfiction, it's important to understand that certain fonts, images (or photographic images) work better for some genres vs. others. Start taking notes of observations as well as things you like or don't like. If you see a cover you like, take a screen shot. The more ideas you collect, the better. This will help you in your decision making.

If you are visiting local bookstores, check to see what bookstores are promoting and showcasing in the front of their stores. Visit the section in the bookstore for your genre to also check out some of the popular books in that area as well.

Refer to Exercise 3b. in the companion workbook where you will find a worksheet to help you search, track and learn from bestselling books.

Book Categories

Another important aspect of book research is understanding book categories. While you are on Amazon, take a look at the book categories for bestselling books. There are a large number of categories available, so you want to make sure you pick the best categories for your book. On an Amazon book listing, scroll down to Product Details, then look at the section called Best Seller's Rank.

Amazon displays the top 3 categories based on the book's activity and sales. Below is an example of the Best Sellers Rank and book categories for *Think and Grow Rich: The Landmark Bestseller Now Revised and Updated for the 21st Century (Think and Grow Rich Series)*:

Best Sellers Rank: #64 in Books (See Top 100 in Books)
#1 in Entrepreneurship (Books)
#1 in Budgeting & Money Management (Books)
#10 in Motivational Self-Help (Books)

Try to find books in your genre with a ranking of less than #5000, which may be an indication that the book is selling well. Note what categories they are in and consider picking the same categories for your book. Let's look at some other examples.

These rankings are from *The Four Agreements: A Practical Guide to Personal Freedom*:

Best Sellers Rank: #1 in Books (See Top 100 in Books)
#1 in New Age & Spirituality
#1 in Psychology & Counseling
#1 in Success Self-Help

These rankings are from one of my technology books, *Microsoft PowerPoint Tips, Tricks and Shortcuts: Presentations, Special Effects and Animations in 25 Mini-Lessons*:

Best Sellers Rank: #330,953 in Kindle Store (See Top 100 in Kindle Store)
#18 in Presentation Software
#55 in Presentation Software Books
#57 in Microsoft PowerPoint Guides

To give you an idea of how things change overtime, the ranking data and format last year for the same technology book was:

Best Sellers Rank: #2,047 Paid in Kindle Store (See Top 100 Paid in Kindle Store)
#14 in Kindle Store > Kindle eBooks > Computers & Technology > Applications & Software > Office Software > Word Processing
#62 in Books > Computers & Technology > Software > Word Processing
#80 in Books > Computers & Technology > Software > Microsoft > Microsoft Word

In the last list of rankings above, notice that the list of categories for my technology book is listed differently. For example, in the last example above, the Word Processing category shows the path of how to get to that category to be: Kindle eBooks > Computers & Technology > Applications & Software > Office Software > Word Processing. However, more recently, I noticed that the full category no longer displayed. I was disappointed to see that Amazon was no longer displaying the breadcrumb trail for each category. Instead, an abbreviated category listing shows. For example, now the category shows as: Word Processing (Kindle Store).

It's important to know how to find the categories for the Best Sellers Rank which is usually nested beneath a plethora of sub-categories. Click on the abbreviated category to see the full path, or breadcrumb trail.

Refer to Exercise 3c. in the companion workbook where you will find a worksheet to help you search, track, and identify bestselling categories.

Keywords

When deciding on the best title and description for your book, it's important to consider search-friendly keywords to make your book more searchable. Here are things you can do to start researching the best keywords for your book:

- Go to Amazon.com > Select "Books" from the list of departments > Start typing a search phrase slowly (for example, type "how to be") -> wait for Amazon to pre-populate a list of potential keywords.
- Go to Google.com > Start typing search words (for example: "10 ways to") > Wait for the autofill function to make suggestions.
- Go to https://keywordtool.io/ which is a free tool used to generate keyword suggestions; statistics including search volume, trend, cost per click (CPC) and other stats are limited, but the tool can still be helpful, and you can upgrade to Keyword Tool Pro if desired.
- Other tools are available (not free) including Kindle Spy (kdspy.com), Publisher Rocket (publisherrocket.com) and KWFinder (kwfinder.com).

Pre-Marketing

When creating your first book, plan to do some pre-marketing tactics way ahead of time. For example, if you are planning a May 1st launch, start spreading the word at least a couple months or more before then, to let potential readers know what's coming and when. If possible, start 6 months to 1 year ahead of time. If you're not sure what your exact launch date will be, it's best to come up with an estimated date. If you keep saying "Coming Soon", readers may lose interest.

Need some suggestions? Read on – this section includes strategies on how you can spread the word about your upcoming book sooner, vs. later.

Build Your Brand

Building your brand is one of the most important things you can do as an author. If you are a celebrity or well-known public figure, people already know you. Why do you think most books written by celebrities are bestselling books overnight? In addition to having a marketing team as well as unlimited marketing funds, people who are well-known already have a large number of followers who trust their opinion. However, most of us are unknown and therefore need to build our brand. You might be wondering if you should pre-market your book or pre-market yourself? In my opinion, it's important to do both. Not only do you want to create buzz online about your book, but you also want to start getting active online and help your audience know more about you. Here are some things you can do ahead of time to help potential readers learn more about "you" as well as your brand:

- Create a logo for your book business and add the logo to your email signature.
- Get a headshot by either booking a photo shoot with a local photographer or ask a good friend to take lots of pictures of you with good lighting (don't use a selfie, which may look unprofessional).

- Share information about your upcoming book on social media including something helpful (free tip sheet, free chapter, advice about an issue, etc.)
- Engage with your audience to learn more about what "they" want and how you can help them (nonfiction) or entertain them (fiction); ask questions, post a survey, etc.

Social Media - Create an Online Presence

Do you have a blog or website? If so, start by posting about your book on one or two of your favorite social media platforms.

Go a step further and create a separate page or website for your book or author journey. When creating a Facebook page, consider creating a business page vs. a personal page, which offers more value such as a Shop Now button, Chat option and integration with your Instagram page. If Facebook is not your thing, there are lots of other social media platforms to consider.

Pre-Order Options

For some of my books, I used the pre-order option available through Kindle Direct Publishing (KDP). If using KDP, this option is only available for eBooks, and not for paperbacks. Although KDP and the self-publishing process isn't covered until later in this book, it's worth mentioning at this time since it's something to consider as a form of pre-marketing. There are pros and cons to using a pre-order option.

Pros:

- Setting up a pre-order allows you to start marketing your book ahead of time, allowing customers to order your not-yet-released book in advance.
- Even though your eBook isn't available for download under the release date, customers can order the eBook anytime leading up to the release date you set, and it will be delivered to them on that date.
- Customers can pre-order your eBook as early as one year before the release date. However, it is not recommended to setup a pre-order for

that far in advance. Instead, a period of 2 to 4 weeks is more common; otherwise, customers may lose interest.

- You can promote your eBook's pre-order page on Author Central, Goodreads, your own site, and elsewhere.
- Pre-orders will contribute toward your sales ranking prior to your eBook's release date, which can help more readers discover your book.

Cons:

- Setting up a pre-order for the eBook version of your book requires that you have several items ready ahead of time as you continue working on your book. This may include your book's front cover design, and a partial draft of your book which you will need to upload. In addition, you may need to prepare marketing materials like book mockups and promotional graphics ahead of time to coincide with your book's pre-order marketing plan.
- You must decide on and select a pre-release date which will be displayed on your Amazon book listing. You can change the release date, but it's best to try to stick to your release date; if you cancel the release of your pre-order book, KDP will suspend your ability to pre-order for one year.
- You cannot update the manuscript file or book details for your eBook within 72 hours of the release. Therefore, if you have last minute changes for your book's go live, you need to upload all necessary files at least four or five days in advance.

You will learn more about KDP in Step 6., where I discuss the self-publishing process which I used for all my books.

Congratulations!

You have now reached the 3rd milestone in your journey!

4

Author Networking

Step 4: Author Networking

Networking Ideas

Whether you are proofing your first draft or have your manuscript completely ready, it's never too soon to start networking. The time is now. Remember like becomes like, so the sooner you network with other writers, authors, and entrepreneurs, the better! Be choosy who you network with too – look for writers in the same genre, who are excited as you are to be an author. If someone brings you down by complaining or posting a negative comment, don't feed into the negativity. Instead, keep it positive, and learn everything you can possibly learn from others. If after you network with someone, you find that you're not learning anything new, then it's a sign to move on. I'm not saying it's time to unfriend the person or unfollow the person altogether and never speak to them again; instead, keep the relationship light and move on to more networking. If one type of networking doesn't work, try something else. The more you network, the greater the chance that you might meet your dream team partner or author network.

Networking With Other Authors

> As I mentioned in Step. 3, joining author groups is one way of getting active online. Let's dive in a little further and discuss more about author networking. When I first started getting serious with my writing, I joined an array of author groups on Facebook; I found that some were more helpful than others. I posted questions, and in some cases, I received instant feedback from other authors. Other types of groups to consider are Writer's Critique Groups (either online or in person), or LinkedIn Groups.

Refer to Exercise 4a. in the companion workbook for an exercise and worksheet on Author Network Tracking.

Sign-Up for Author Events

➢ Sign-up and attend author expos and book events: I would recommend searching for local author expos at libraries, bookstores, and other establishments. This is a wonderful opportunity to showcase your books. In addition, you get to meet and talk to other authors as well. Author expos at libraries are usually free or very inexpensive. I've been signing up for author expos at local libraries for the past several years. I also signed up for a couple outdoor book festivals; although it did require that I invest in a folding table and outdoor tent, it turned out to be a very positive and profitable experience. In 2019, when searching online, I discovered an opportunity for story time reading for my children's books in a nearby shopping center pavilion; I contacted the manager and they were looking for authors to volunteer for readings, so I signed up. 2020 was not a good year for author events, but things picked up in 2021 and beyond.

Share Information

➢ Create a section on your blog to interview other authors and share information. I created an Author's Corner page on my blog and started interviewing other authors. Interviewing doesn't have to be a lot of work. You can come up with a series of questions to ask other authors; they can fill in the answers and return the sheet to you electronically. If you prefer, you can interview them on video and post the video on your blog or YouTube channel. The Authors Helping Authors section in this chapter includes 12 author interviews.

➢ Spread the word about your book, create a flyer, info sheet, or promotional graphic and ask others to Like and Share.

➢ Create a landing page and offer a free chapter to anyone who signs-up. In addition to the free chapter, include a cliff hanger or something to whet their appetite about your book. This helps your build your email list so you can notify potential readers and tell them about your book at go live.

Build a Book Launch Team

> What is a book launch team? It's a group of individuals who are interested in receiving a free, advanced copy of your book so they can review and provide feedback. They may also provide a testimonial for you which you can use in your marketing materials. Ideally, your launch team should consist of individuals who are generally interested in your book and spreading the word about your book. Although it's helpful to have a large book launch team, even a small group of 15 to 20 people is helpful.

> Remember that not everyone who promises to read your book will actually read it. It's important to send reminder emails to your launch team to follow-up and make sure they read it as well as post a review.

> When you launch your book, consider having one or more promotion days at launch and offer your eBook for free. Ask everyone on your launch team to purchase your book for free on Amazon at launch. This will not only boost your sales ranking, but when they post a review for you, they will be doing so as a verified purchaser of your book. If you don't want to offer your book for free, you can initially price it at .99 cents, then slowly increase the price during the first week. Aim at getting at least 10 reviews during the first week of your book launch. You can also summarize reviews and include them on your website or blog.

Other Networking

Here are some additional strategies for author networking:

> Follow authors in your genre on Amazon – learn from other authors.

> Register for an online author event and ask a lot of questions.

> Attend an author event at a library or bookshop – mix and mingle.

> Join writing organizations – if you are just starting out, the least expensive ones are online groups; there are larger organizations such as the Author Guild, or the Society of Children's Book Writers and Illustrators (for children's book authors) but the latter does have yearly membership fees.

> Be more proactive online – join and engage in more author groups.

> Do a joint promotion or joint giveaway with another author – once you find an author or two in your genre, collaborate and create a giveaway event to share to both of your audiences.

Authors Helping Authors - Interviews

Over the years, I have met authors of all kinds, who wrote in all different genres. I met authors who were just starting out as well as seasoned authors. I met authors who wrote one book, a few books, or dozens of books! The most interesting aspect of attending in-person author events during that time was meeting and talking with authors and hearing their stories of how they got started, what inspired them to write and what their books were about. Every author event I attended was more fun than the last.

The following interviews were authors I have met during my journey. I met some in person, and some online. They live both near and far, and they all have an interesting story to tell about how they started writing and how they became an author.

Special Thanks to:

Ellwyn Autumn
Pooja Chilukuri
Ann Harrison
H. Corinne Hewitt
James Hockenberry
Jen Lowry
Donna L Martin
Karen Scheuer
Steve Scott
Judy Stavisky
Jeni Temen
Heidi Thorne

Ellwyn Autumn, Children's Book Author

In 2018, I had the pleasure of meeting Ellwyn Autumn at a local Author Expo. We quickly shared our marketing ideas as we discussed our love of writing and self-publishing books. In 2019, we worked together, offering story time readings in our local community. Thank you, Ellwyn for taking the time for this author interview.

Amelia: Tell us about yourself and how many books you've written.

Ellwyn: I'm a former Pre-Kindergarten/Kindergarten teacher. I taught for twenty years, 17 of them were with The School District of Philadelphia. Nowadays, I write children's books, blog, and write book reviews on Lemon Drop Literary.

Amelia: What is your latest book and what inspired it?

Ellwyn: My most recently published book is a children's book called *Teddy Bear Tea*.

Amelia: What authors or books have influenced you?

Ellwyn: J.K Rowling is my all-time favorite author. Her Harry Potter Series will forever be my number one series to read. The worldbuilding and character development in the stories are superb. But what I enjoy most about her books is the way she writes. Her word choices and descriptions are genius! Another favorite author of mine is Jan Brett. Her picture book illustrations are phenomenal.

Amelia: What are you working on now?

Ellwyn: I'm reviewing books on Lemon Drop Literary and writing a story about a wizard who works in a hospital. I don't have a title yet.

Amelia: What is your best method to promote books?

Ellwyn: To be honest, I'm still figuring this out. I find marketing and promotion quite tricky. From what I've learned, an email list is one of the best ways to spread the word about your work.

Amelia: What advice do you have for new authors?

Ellwyn: Read, write, repeat! After that, join a writer's group and be open to an honest critique. If you're serious about developing your craft, you must listen and follow through with people's suggestions for improvement. Write what you know, and what you're passionate about.

Ellwyn's Bio:

Ellwyn Autumn is an American author/blogger/ghostwriter and a certified teacher with a Master's Degree in Education. She writes children's picture books, middle-grade novels, and Young Adult fiction.

Ellwyn's first self-published novel, *Chris Kringle's Cops The First Mission*, was a Finalist in the 2016 Reader's Favorite International Book Contest. Her Kamyla Chung picture book series addresses difficult issues facing young children. *Kamyla Chung and the Classroom Bully* is on Jedlie's Certified Great Reads List and earned Story Monster Approval.

Ellwyn discovered her passion for writing in second grade when she had to write a book report for school. She was so excited to write the report, until her mother told her that she had to write about someone else's book and not her own story. Ellwyn became indignant and decided that once she finished the book report she would most certainly write her own original story. She has been writing ever since!

Ellwyn lives with her family in Pennsylvania. She loves all things magical, curling up with a good book, writing stories, and almost anything with chocolate in it.

Ellwyn's Social Media Links:

Website: www.ellwynautumn.com

Blog: lemondropliterary.blogspot.com

Pooja Chilukuri, Nutritional Therapy Practitioner (NTP), Health Coach, and Author

Pooja and I met through an online author group and quickly began networking and sharing ideas about our author journeys. Thank you, Pooja, for taking the time to let me interview you today.

Amelia: Tell us about yourself and how many books you have written.

Pooja: I am a Nutritional Therapy Practitioner and Health Coach. In addition, I am passionate about health and wellness education and for being a voice for those who have experienced religious wounds that stem from distorted images of God and/or "church hurt". I have written five books (4 print books and 1 e-book) which include my memoir (my journey of recovering from religion and discovering myself), reflections/devotional books and a guidebook for using supplements wisely.

Amelia: What is the name of your latest book and what inspired it?

Pooja: My latest faith-based books are the *Unveiling Jesus* series. It was inspired by the many stories of people who felt stuck in religious systems where they developed distorted images of Jesus, codependent relationships with God and church leaders. The devotionals were birthed from a desire to break free from "in-the-box" thinking of Jesus and use the gospel stories as a tool to reflect on his heart. My nutrition book is inspired by my working with those who are beginning their health journey and feel overwhelmed and confused about where to begin and what information to trust as they navigate the online world for answers.

Amelia: What authors, or books have influenced you?

Pooja: Elizabeth Gilbert's *Big Magic* has inspired me on my author journey. Also, I also love reading Agatha Christie's work. Max Lucado's writing style and content are also inspiring.

Amelia: What are you working on now?

Pooja: I am working on historical fiction (trying a new genre, a series). It will be my first experiment with fiction.

Amelia: What is your best method to promote your books?

Pooja: Thus far it has been through social media and networking. I will be experimenting with Goodreads soon.

Amelia: Do you have any advice for new authors?

Pooja: Your story/message is important, as Elizabeth Gilbert said, "It may have been done before but it has not been done by you." Writing has aptly been referred to as a 'solo sport', but it takes a team to birth a book. Having a support system (family, writing groups, beta readers, etc.) can help! As you develop your craft, do not forget to keep the art in your writing alive and above all else, stay with the love for writing.

Bio: Pooja Chilukuri is a Nutritional Therapy Practitioner (NTP), Health Coach, and a published author. Pooja's mission is to empower individuals to navigate the often-confusing nutrition and health trends and take charge of their health to prevent chronic illnesses from taking a toll. In 2015, Pooja published her memoir, *And Then There Was Jesus* where she shares her journey of recovering from religion, healing from spiritual wounds and discovering herself. Her other books, *Unveiling Jesus Through His Passion*; *Unveiling Jesus Through His Incarnation* and *Once There Was Jesus* seek to uncover the heart of Jesus through the gospel stories. She is also the author of the e-book, *A Beginner's Guide to Using Supplements*.

Pooja's Social Media Sites:

Amazon Author Page: http://amazon.com/author/poojachilukuri

Website: http://www.poojachilukuri.com

Facebook: http://www.facebook.com/AuthorPoojaChilukuri

Ann Harrison, Author and Podcaster

Ann Harrison is the author of four books, including *The Spirit of Creativity: Inspirational Poems for the Creative at Heart*, *Maggie's Gravy Train Adventure*, *Inner Vision*, and *A Journey of Faith: A Stepping Stones Mystery*, which is currently under revision. Thank you, Ann, for taking the time to allow me to interview you today.

Amelia: Tell us about yourself and how many books you have written.

Ann: I am an author, a freelance writer and I run a podcast called Inspirational Journeys. When I'm not writing or podcasting, I love to sit out on my front porch and listen to my wind chimes while brainstorming. I've written several books, but four of them are currently published. Three of which I'm promoting, and one I'm rewriting.

Amelia: What is the name of your latest book and what inspired it?

Ann: My latest book is entitled *The Spirit of Creativity: Inspirational Poems for the Creative at Heart*. A friend inspired me to start focusing on my poetry writing through prompts she shared on her podcast. However, the Holy Spirit gave me many of my poems, while a few poems here and there, were inspired by other writing prompts. Most of my poetry comes to me when I'm sitting out on my front porch.

Amelia: What authors, or books have influenced you?

Ann: Jen Lowry, Terri Blackstock, Karen Kingsbury, Janette Oke, and so many throughout my life.

Amelia: What are you working on now?

Ann: As I mentioned above, I'm rewriting my novel entitled *A Journey of Faith: A Stepping Stones Mystery*. I thought I only had four books in this series, but it's bigger than I could have ever imagined.

Amelia: What is your best method to promote your books?

Ann: To be honest, I'm still working on that one. I put my links up on social media when people in the writing community ask for them, or as pieces in specific threads or using the hashtag #ShamelessSelfPromotion in certain Facebook groups. I have also put the latest one on a couple of promotion websites. However, for the most part, I talk about my process on my podcast.

Amelia: Do you have any advice for new authors?

Ann: Listen to the experts, but be mindful of what works for you. The writing process isn't a one size fits all approach and each person's process is different.

Ann's Bio: In addition to writing four books, Ann has also been published in several anthologies and she contributed to a devotional entitled *God Things: Hope for the Hurting*, alongside Jen Lowry and fifteen other authors. Aside from her work as a Christian fiction author, Ann is a professional freelance writer. She also hosts the Inspirational Journeys Podcast, where she gives authors, creative artists and entrepreneurs a platform to share their stories. When she's not interviewing special guests, she hosts solo episodes providing book reviews, reading selected poems, and sharing tips and encouragement for aspiring authors.

Ann's Social Media Sites:

- Website: https://annwritesinspiration.com
- Book Link: https://books2read.com/TheSpiritOfCreativity
- Facebook: https://www.facebook.com/annwritesinspiration
- Pinterest: https://www.pinterest.com/annwritesinspiration
- Twitter: https://twitter.com/annwrites75
- YouTube: https://www.youtube.com/user/annsmusic1
- Podcast: https://anchor.fm/inspirational-journeys

H. Corinne Hewitt, Author and Quilt Shop Owner

H. Corinne Hewitt (H. C. Hewitt author name) and I met online via an author's group and share a fondness of writing and cooking. Corinne is a quilter by day and an author by night. Welcome, Corinne and thank you for allowing me to interview you today!

Amelia: Tell us about yourself and how many books you have written.

Corinne: Hello, I am a businesswoman, and I have owned my own quilt shop for almost twelve years now in the town of Hanna, Alberta. I have been married for thirty-one years and have four grown-up children and six grandchildren. I love to do many things, quilting, design quilt patterns, baking, fiddling, chalk painting, art quilts, junk journals, antique collecting, and best of all writing books. I have written five books, three novels, one cookbook, and one Bible study (which coincides with my first novel). All of my books are in *The Abbington Pickets Series*, beginning with *Jacob of Abbington Pickets*.

Amelia: What is the name of your latest book and what inspired it?

Corinne: *Letters from Jacob* is the latest one, and is a continuation in the series of Abbington Pickets. The whole series is inspired by the Victorian historical village I grew up near, where my grandma worked at for eighteen years. I got to go there and tell people the history of the village and area just like she did. She even let me dress up, as she did. I loved that place so much I said I wanted to write a fiction book about it.

Amelia: What authors, or books have influenced you?

Corinne: I loved *Anne of Green Gables* as a teen and researched L. M. Montgomery, I was intrigued by her story. I loved *Little Women*, *Little Men* and *Jo's Boys* by Louisa May Alcott as well. And who doesn't love *Gone with the Wind*? I can't say any particular author made me decide to write a book, I always wanted to pen my story, and thought authors were the most famous and wonderful people in the world and I wanted to be one of them!

Amelia: What are you working on now?

Corinne: Right now, I am writing the fourth novel in the series, *Jacob's Secret*, and after that I will be back at writing *Earnestly Waiting* which will be part of the series, with another character, named Ernest, from the second and third novels. Also, with my co-author, Karma Goodbrand, we will be doing another Bible study this year to coincide with my second book, *Jacob's Place*.

Amelia: What is your best method to promote your books?

Corinne: I do have all my books available online, such as Amazon, Chapters, Barnes and Noble and my website, but the best way I sell them is through my quilt store. I designed quilt patterns that relate to my novels and that helps with selling the book as well.

Amelia: Do you have any advice for new authors?

Corinne: Just start and don't stop until you're done your first draft. Don't ever give up! I was there once, and I remember how I knew nothing. In a hurry you learn a lot! Persistence is key.

Corinne's Bio: H. C. Hewitt grew up on a farm in southeastern Saskatchewan, where she developed a deep appreciation for the rural prairie landscape and the people who live there. She has been passionate about reading and writing from an early age and always knew that she would someday write a historical romance. Her grandmother's extensive knowledge of Saskatchewan history and her grandfather's collection of antiques sparked an enduring love of history, especially of the era in which her story unfolds. Her story's setting, in the series of Abbington Pickets, was inspired by a historic park near where she grew up, founded in 1882 by an Englishman who set out to create a Victorian village in Canada. H. C. Hewitt's other passion is quilting; she owns and operates a quilt shop, where she designs and makes quilt patterns. Her four children have grown up and moved away, giving her more time for writing and quilting. She also has six grandchildren and loves to spend time with them. H. C. Hewitt lives in rural eastern central Alberta with her husband, dog, two cats, and nine miniature donkeys.

Corinne's Social Media Sites:

- www.hchewittauthor.com
- @hchewittauthor for Facebook, Instagram and Twitter

James Hockenberry, MBA, Author

I would like to introduce you to James Hockenberry, MBA. James and I met at an author expo author event held at a local library. Welcome, James and thank you for allowing me to interview you today.

Amelia: Tell us about yourself and how many books you have written.

James: I'm a retired financial executive who has reinvented himself as a writer of World War I thrillers. I've self-published three award winning books in my trilogy: *Over Here* (covering German sabotage in American during 1915-16), *So Beware* (focusing on the 1919 Paris Peace Talks), and now *Send the Word* (centering on the U.S. military experience on the Western Front in 1918).

Amelia: What is the name of your latest book and what inspired it?

James: My latest book *Send the Word*, was released in 2020. It is the 3rd book in my WWI intrigue Series; I've always been fascinated on military history and stories of life-and-death: what I call "Man at his brink". It is inspired by real events as I try to dramatize key events in America's involvement in World War I.

Amelia: What authors, or books have influenced you?

James: Louis Uris, Ken Follett, James Mitchener, and Frederick Forsyth

Amelia: What are you working on now?

James: Now that my 3rd book, *Send the Word*, has been independently published, I'm working on promoting my book. I have an idea for a 4th WWI story, outside of the Trilogy, but I have much research and character / plot development to do first.

Amelia: What is your best method to promote your books?

James: Personal events, particularly historical lectures on WWI. I've entered a number of books contests, and the awards I've won give my books credibility and exposure. I have a handout of interesting facts for each of the books I've written, and I give these away for free. I always say, "We don't sell our books first. We sell ourselves."

Amelia: Do you have any advice for new authors?

James:

- Learn by doing.
- Respect the craft.
- Keep writing, don't be discouraged.
- Write because you love it.
- Write about what you want to know about.
- Don't be afraid to take chances.
- Physically visit the places you are writing about.

Bio: I grew up in the Westchester suburbs of New York City. With an MBA from Columbia University, I followed a career in operational finance until I left Corporate America at age 55. I have now reinvented myself as a World War I thriller writer and often say, "The journey is the reward." Writing books is the most challenging thing I've ever done intellectually. It's great fun too.

James's Website: http://www.jameshockenberry.com

Jen Lowry, Literary Coach, Author Coach, Teacher and Author

I would like to introduce you to Dr. Jennifer Ikner Lowry. Jen and I met through an author group and found that we have a lot in common, including writing in different genres and wearing different hats, all leading back to books. Welcome, Jen and thank you for allowing me to interview you today.

Amelia: Tell us about yourself and how many books you have written.

Jen: I'm a Literacy Coach for Wake County Schools, Author Coach, Homeschool "momma" by night, publisher of Monarch Educational Services, L.L.C., and author all the times in between. I've published twenty books and counting, with the platform, *Clean Books for All Ages*.

Amelia: What is the name of your latest book and what inspired it?

Jen: *Love Over Pizza* was published on January 25, 2021, and was inspired by my true love story. I met my husband online and creating a cast of characters, an online dating site, and all of the thrills and stress that comes with all of that piled on with grief, friendship, and pizza was one of my favorite books to write.

Amelia: What authors or books have influenced you?

Jen: The first book that really spoke to me as an author was *A Walk to Remember* by Nicholas Sparks. When I first read it, I said, "I want to do this." I started writing in 8th grade, but never took it seriously until that book. I've never looked back. Kate DiCamillo is also my favorite author, and with each reread of her novels, it inspires me to write about hope. So many books inspire me that I could spend hours talking with you about them!

Amelia: What are you working on now?

Jen: I'm super excited to share that my first thriller, police procedural novel, *The Sunday Killer*, will be released by City Limits Publishing in 2021! My Aunt Dot named the character, Heather Moody. I can't wait for people to meet my detective and hope this becomes book one of many in a series from her case files.

Amelia: What is your best method to promote your books?

Jen: My podcast, Jen Lowry Writes, has been an amazing way to connect with readers and other writers. I would've never imagined I'd build a strong platform with sharing out my author journey with others. It's a blessing to have a writing community, so I challenge you to join or create one. Author friendships are powerful!

Amelia: Do you have any advice for new authors?

Jen: Don't stop writing. Don't get discouraged. Honor your blank page and build your author community as you go. This life is a calling, not a hobby. It's about following your passions and learning as you go. There's always a starting place with everything we do in life. Get started today and embrace the challenges as they come.

Bio: Jen Lowry lives outside of Raleigh, North Carolina and is a proud native of Robeson County. She is the author of a YA contemporary fiction novel, *Sweet Potato Jones* (2020 with *Swoon Romance*) and a list of other bestselling novels. Check out her twenty published books and counting. You'll find her enjoying every second of life spent with her family (preferably in pajamas). If you ask her what she's reading it's probably more than one book. Learn more about Jen at http://www.jenlowrywrites.com and follow her online @jenlowrywrites.

Jen's Social Media Sites:

Website: http://www.jenlowrywrites.com

Facebook: https://www.facebook.com/jenlowrywrites

Donna L Martin, Author and 4th Degree Black Belt in TaeKwonDo

Donna L Martin is the author of 10 books, and she has more books coming soon. I had the pleasure of meeting Donna through an online author's group, and we quickly found that we had a lot in common. We both enjoy reading and writing in different genres, and the mascot in her HISTORY'S MYSTERIES book series is named Amelia Earmouse. What a lovely name for a mascot! Thank you, Donna, for taking the time to allow me to interview you today.

Amelia: Tell us about yourself and how many books you have written.

Donna: I have been writing for over 45 years, but professionally for only 10 years. When I'm not running my martial arts school, I'm writing books in a number of genres, including inspirational, picture books, historical fiction chapter books, and young adult fantasy. The last ten years have been good to me. I have ten books published as of 2020. I have three more books scheduled to be released throughout 2021.

Amelia: What is the name of your latest book and what inspired it?

Donna: My latest book, *HISTORY'S MYSTERIES: Hunting Gris-Gris*, was released March 2020. It was inspired by my love of both uncovering little known historical events and encouraging children to explore the past.

Amelia: What authors, or books have influenced you?

Donna: I have an extremely eclectic taste in reading. My reading list includes everything from Mercer Mayer's Little Critter series, all the way to nonfiction like books exploring the assassination of President Lincoln. I read Reader's Digest to stay up to date with a variety of topics and read over 200 picture books and chapter books every summer to gage the latest industry trends. A great story that touches me can come from any genre, so I enjoy them all.

Amelia: What are you working on now?

Donna: I've almost completed the research for book four of my *HISTORY'S MYSTERIES: President Lincoln's Balloons*. It will take place during the Civil War and allows me to introduce my readers to the men who helped the North win the war from high in the sky. It's scheduled to be released by Story Catcher Publishing by the summer of 2022.

Amelia: What is your best method to promote your books?

Donna: I do everything from author visits, Facebook promos, bookmarks, postcards, Instagram advertising, library visits, emails, newsletters, and school visits. They all are good methods for me, depending on the particular readers I'm trying to reach...sometimes librarians, bookstores, teachers, children, parents, etc.

Amelia: Do you have any advice for new authors?

Donna: Have a plan. Fine-tune your goals. Write the strongest story you can and then build the best network you can to give you feedback on how to make that story even stronger. Research your genre so you know exactly what the world expects from your story. Know your publishing options and don't skimp on your cover. Attend as many physical or online workshops as you can and never stop learning how to improve your storytelling skills.

Donna's Bio: Best-selling, award-winning author, Donna L Martin, has been writing since she was eight years old. She is a 4th Degree Black Belt in TaeKwonDo by day and a 'ninja' writer of flash fiction, children's picture books, chapter books, young adult novels and inspirational essays by night. Donna is a BOOK NOOK REVIEWS host providing the latest book reviews on all genres of children's books, and the host of WRITERLY WISDOM, a resource series for writers. Donna is a member of the Society of Children's Book Writers & Illustrators and Children's Book Insider. She is a lover of dark chocolate, going to the beach and adding to her growing book collection.

Donna's Social Media Sites:

- Website: www.storycatcherpublishing.com
- Facebook: www.facebook.com/donasdays
- Twitter: www.twitter.com/donasdays
- Amazon: www.amazon.com/author/donnalmartin

Karen Scheuer, Author and Retired Elementary Teacher/Professor

In 2018, I had the pleasure of meeting Karen Scheuer at a local Author Expo. In addition to being a children's book author, Karen also creates beautiful calligraphy. Thank you, Karen, for taking the time for this author interview.

Amelia: Tell us about yourself and how many books you have written.

Karen: I am a retired elementary school teacher, and a retired professor. I currently have two books I have published. *A Bug and a Wish*, is a story about bullying. In 2019, I released my second book, which is called *I Know Something You Don't Know*. It's a guessing book for young children. I originally wrote it while in high school, when I was 17 years old.

Amelia: What inspired you to write your book?

Karen: In regards to my book, *A Bug and a Wish*, as an elementary teacher, I wanted a way to introduce students to use powerful words to prevent teasing and bullying.

Amelia: What authors, or books have influenced you?

Karen: I like books for kids which teach a lesson.

Amelia: What is your best method to promote your books?

Karen: Amazon is serving my book well. I do some author expos if the table is free or inexpensive.

Amelia: Do you have any advice for new authors?

Karen: Don't wait to publish your book, and get started right away.

Amelia: Is there anything else you would to share to readers and other authors?

Karen: I love doing school visits where I read my book to the kids and do an anti-bullying activity. I live in Newtown, PA. I used my kids' names as the two main characters in my book. I'm glad my book can empower kids.

Karen's Social Media Sites:

- www.SBPRAbooks.com/KarenScheuer
- www.amazon.com/author/karenscheuer

Steve Scott, Wall Street Journal Bestselling Author and Course Instructor

I would like to introduce you to Steve Scott. Years ago, when I started getting serious about writing and start self-publishing, I discovered an online course called Authority Pub Academy (APA) and Steve was one of the instructors and creators of the course. Steve's course literally changed my life, and I would not be where I am today if it wasn't for the APA course. Steve is also a bestselling author of over 100 books. Welcome, Steve and thank you for allowing me to interview you today.

Amelia: Tell us about yourself and how many books you have written.

Steve: I got into self-publishing back in 2012 as an extra way to promote my blog content. But I quickly fell in love with the platform and the numerous opportunities that it offered. I focused on self-publishing full-time in 2013 and it has been my primary focus up until last year (when I started experimenting with other platforms). At this point, I have 111 books on Amazon. Some are in my "habit line" of books. Others are small books that I experimented with back in 2013. And a few are part of foreign translations or book bundles.

Amelia: What is the name of your latest book and what inspired it?

Steve: *Stack Your Savings* written with Rebecca Livermore. Lately, I have been fascinated with the financial independence (FI) concept where people focus on retiring years, even decades, before the standard retirement age. One major FI concept is how small adjustments you make to your daily spending can quickly add up – especially if you put that money into index funds through the Vanguard website. We wrote *Stack Your Savings* to provide a detailed list of the small and large strategies you can use to cut down your monthly expenses. Our hope is this will provide readers with a list of step-by-step actions they can use to save more and put this money toward their important goals.

Amelia: What authors, or books have influenced you?

Steve: I have three books that have influenced me heavily:

#1. Principles of Success by Jack Canfield

This book contains 67 principles that are important for success. Each principle has a variety of compelling stories and anecdotes, but the real value comes from the specific actions and habits you can use to improve any aspect of your life. It's the first book that showed how success in life really comes down to your choice in daily habits.

#2. The Millionaire Fastlane by MJ Demarco

I'll admit that this book has a bit of a "get-rich-quick" title, but it's the best business mindset book that I've ever read. What Demarco emphasizes is to build a business that's free from your personal time. Specifically, I learned the value of creating "digital assets" that generate income even when I don't work.

#3. The One Thing by Gary Keller and Jay Papasan

The basic idea is that you don't need to do dozens of things in order to be successful. Instead, if you simplify your business (and life) to what's essential, then you will achieve great results – in often half the time that it takes others.

The big lesson that I pulled from this book is to schedule time for the #1 priority daily related to your goal. Until you've completed this daily action, nothing else should get your attention. Bonus points if you do it first thing in the morning.

Amelia: What are you working on now?

Steve: Although I'm working on a couple of books (mostly related to mindfulness), I'm also in the process of building up a YouTube channel where I can focus on a variety of topics like productivity, habit development, self-publishing, and running an online business.

Amelia: What is your best method to promote your books?

Steve: Building an email list! Marketing to an email list helps you:

#1. Provide additional value to readers. You can give them extras like PDFs that help them take action on the principles you teach, videos that demonstrate a specific technique, and resources where they can additional information.

#2. Generate reviews from your street team. You can segment your "superfans" into a separate email list where they receive advance copies of your book. In return, you ask them to leave a review when it is launched.

#3. Promote books when they're launched. You can generate a surge of sales once whenever you publish a new book. Not only does this produce income, but it also helps your book rank well on Amazon, which leads to more sales from people who aren't part of your email list.

#4. Build other brands. If you want to start another brand (like a blog, podcast, or YouTube channel), then you can leverage these followers to create initial buzz and get traction on that platform. Since subscribers already like your books, they will probably like the other types of media that you create.

Amelia: Do you have any advice for new authors?

Steve: Couple of things:

#1. Find a niche and make sure it's profitable. The strategy that I recommend is to look on Amazon and make sure people buy books about this topic. I like to look at the "Amazon Best Seller's Rank" (or ASBR) of similar books. If I see multiple books with a rank of #30,000 or less, then I know it's probably a profitable niche.

#2. Go inch wide, mile deep. Most readers don't have time to read massive compendiums that cover an entire market. Instead, they prefer short, actionable books that provide an extensive solution on one strategy. Put simply, your book should focus on a single topic in your market, which provides an extensive solution to this challenge.

#3. Write multiple books in this market. The quickest ways to build momentum on a self-publishing platform is to continuously write for your specific market. With that in mind, I recommend you go back to your audience to discover:

- What other problems do they have?
- What strategies from your first book need to be fleshed out?
- What challenges are you seeing from your research that haven't been answered?

#4. Run AMS ads. Amazon Marketing Services (or AMS) is a great platform for marketing your books to readers. That's why, I suggest you focus on mastering this ads platform. The trick is to do extensive research and find hundreds, even thousands of keywords for each of your books.

You should look for three types of keywords: 1. Similar book titles, 2. Author names, and 3. Problem-centric phrases (like "how to ___"). Start at a $0.30 bid and keep tweaking your ads and cost-per-click until you find a few "winners" that you can scale up.

Steve's Social Media Sites:

Steve's Website: https://www.developgoodhabits.com

Steve YouTube Channels:

http://youtube.com/user/developgoodhabits

https://www.youtube.com/channel/UCuo-ccyhxSv5wwWxRl_0W5w

Steve's Amazon Author Page: https://www.amazon.com/author/sjscott

Bio: Steve Scott is a Wall Street Journal bestselling author with over 100 books in his catalog. He also blogs about habit development on his site DevelopGoodHabits.com and creates videos on his YouTube channel. When not working, S.J. likes to read, exercise, travel and spend time with his family.

Judy Stavisky, MPH, M.Ed., Author

I would like to introduce you to Judy Stavisky, MPH, M.Ed. Judy and I met at an author expo event held at a local library. Welcome, Judy and thank you for allowing me to interview you today.

Amelia: Tell us about yourself and how many books you have written.

Judy: I have written my first book with Sister Constance Touey and Sister Jeannette Lucey. Our book chronicles the journeys of immigrants and refugees who were welcomed to the United States by the predominantly African American students at a Catholic School in West Philadelphia, Pennsylvania.

Amelia: What is the name of your latest book and what inspired it?

Judy: My latest book is entitled: *Do It Better! How the Kids of St. Frances de Sales Exceeded Everyone's Expectations*. Sister Constance Touey and Sister Jeannette Lucey, IHM are two tenacious nuns who wrapped their arms around children who suffered unspeakable losses and launched them on a path to success. Not just a few children, but hundreds of students from around the world arrived at their Catholic School and were welcomed. Fiercely devoted to their students, we have written a moving and evocative book that chronicles the students' triumphs over adversity. Do It Better! offers hope and optimism amidst today's divisive conversations about immigrants and refugees.

Amelia: What are you working on now?

Judy: A non-fiction book about the lives of Amish women. I have been visiting with Amish women and their families for the past seven years. I have learned that a life of hard work and simplicity is often anything but simple.

Amelia: What is your best method to promote your books?

Judy: College Alumni Newsletters and regional magazines, educational newsletters, bookstore readings, and presentations at senior living residences.

Amelia: Do you have any advice for new authors?

Judy: Try to secure a book review in a local community online or print newspaper, include the name of your book in your e-mail signature (you never know who might be interested in your topic), and contact anyone you have ever met who might be interested in the topic you are covering.

Bio: Judy is on the faculty of the Drexel Dornsife School of Public Health and a Senior Advisor to several non-profit organizations specializing in community outreach and organizational development. Judy's interest in Amish women and their families has led her on a seven year quest to more clearly understand and document the riddle of Amish life.

Website: TheWelcomeSchool.com

Jeni Temen, Author and Former Real Estate Broker/Investor

Jeni and I met through an online author group and quickly began networking and sharing ideas about our author journeys. Thank you, Jeni, for taking the time to let me interview you today.

Amelia: Tell us about yourself and how many books you have written.

Jeni: I'm a former long time real estate broker and real estate investor. I published 3 books so far and have several others in the works.

Amelia: What is the name of your latest book and what inspired it?

Jeni: My latest book is called *Credit+Budget=Control: Improve your life immediately!* My other books include: *How To Buy A Home That Makes You Happy. Don't just buy a house, buy a home!* and *For Sale By Owner, It's not rocket science, just follow the rules.*

I wrote the real estate books to help anyone who wants to buy or sell a home to make an informed decision. Over my long career, I learned that many people are making decisions based on their realtor, loan officer, or other helpful people's opinion when buying or selling their most valuable asset. The books are giving readers a guide to proceed in ways that is beneficial to them, according to their own circumstances.

Amelia: What authors, or books have influenced you?

Jeni: I was influenced by the lack of books written for consumers. There are many books about Real Estate on the market, but they all are written for agents, not for their clients.

Amelia: What are you working on now?

Jeni: I am working on a credit repair step by step class and book. A manual with forms and guidance on how to repair your credit just like an attorney or credit repair business does it.

Amelia: What is your best method to promote your books?

Jeni: So far, I use Amazon to promote my books by sharing my book links on social media.

Amelia: Do you have any advice for new authors?

Jeni: My advice is to learn how to submit and where to submit the book to be published before it's published. Hiring others to help you can be a VERY costly mistake, so it's important to do your research first. The more you learn about how to self publish, the better. Through trial and error, you can learn the best methods and save a lot of time.

Jeni's Social Media Sites:

- Website: www.RMoneyClub.com
- Facebook: www.facebook.com/RMoneyClub
- Amazon Author Page: www.amazon.com/author/jenitemen

Heidi Thorne, Author and Host of the Heidi Thorne Show Podcast

I would like to introduce you to Heidi Thorne, who is a business nonfiction author and host of The Heidi Thorne Show podcast where she discusses self-publishing. Welcome, Heidi and thank you for allowing me to interview you today.

Amelia: Tell us about yourself and how many books you have written.

Heidi: I'm a nonfiction business author and podcaster. My main topics are self-publishing and small business. I have self-published over 20 books.

Amelia: What is the name of your latest book and what inspired it?

Heidi: *Networking for Authors: How to Build Your Fan Base and Book Sales through Networking* (available on Amazon, Audible, and Apple Books)

Amelia: What authors or books have influenced you?

Heidi: Hands down, it's business author and philosopher, Seth Godin. His work makes you think differently and clearly.

Amelia: What are you working on now?

Heidi: I'm concentrating on building my YouTube channel and podcast where I discuss publishing issues.

Amelia: What is your best method to promote your books?

Heidi: I believe the best way to promote your books is by building and engaging with your author platform, or fan base, on social media. I also use Amazon ads. Amazon advertising worked much better years ago. It can be competitive, so it takes some experimenting over time to see positive results. I have several Amazon ad campaigns that I run continuously for my backlist titles.

Amelia: Do you have any advice for new authors?

Heidi: Decide if a book is really the best way to get your message to your target audience, vs. a blog, which may be a better starting point. In addition to a blog, you can consider a YouTube channel, podcast, events, online courses, or social media. It's important to realize that initially, your book will not be your major source of income. This depends on how much you invest in advertising and networking. My survey research of self-published authors found that 73% make less than $1,000 a year from their books. The bottom line is to be very clear about what you hope to accomplish with your self-publishing efforts.

Heidi's Bio: In addition to self-publishing, Heidi was a trade newspaper editor and advertising manager for 15 years. Heidi owned an imprinted promotional products business for 17 years. In sum, she has been in advertising, sales, and publishing for over 25 years. In addition, she taught at the college level for 5 years in adult career and computer education.

Heidi's Social Media Sites:

- Website: https://heidithorne.com
- Amazon Author Page: https://amazon.com/author/heidithorne

Congratulations!

You have now reached the 4th milestone in your journey!

5

The Formatting and Editing Process

Step 5: The Formatting and Editing Process

The Formatting Process

At this point in the journey, I hope you have the first draft of your manuscript completed. As I mentioned earlier in this book, it's best to write first and edit later. Editing too much before you get all the words down may interfere with the creative process.

The software I use when writing, composing, and editing is Microsoft Word. This is a matter of preference, and you can certainly use another software program to write content. You just want to make sure that the software you use has all the features you need for book formatting.

You can also use notebooks and journals when writing, but ultimately you will need to have an electronic version of your manuscript. Although I do use lots of notebooks and journals for creative writing, and for when ideas pop into my head, when I'm composing content for my books, I typically type directly on my computer in Microsoft Word.

As I mentioned before, I love different types of journals and notebooks, and I especially like to keep a notebook in the family room and a mini notebook on my nightstand in my bedroom. I cannot tell you how many times I woke up in the middle of the night, or laid in bed, tossing – with ideas that I didn't know what to do with – and some nights I didn't have my little notebook or journal handy. I tried to remember the idea in the morning but it's just not the same.

In this chapter, I'll explain the process I use to edit and format my content. Even if you are considering hiring an editor and proofreader to help you format your manuscript, you can still benefit by understanding the process necessary to turn your raw manuscript into a formatted masterpiece.

Although I will be referencing Microsoft Word for the interior formatting, if you are using a different software program, not to worry – you should still be able to apply *most* of the editing features in other programs, but there are exceptions. This depends on the capabilities of the other software tools.

Refining Your Outline

Earlier in this book, in Step 2. The Writing Process, I recommended that you write an outline to help you lay out the sections and chapters of your book. At this point, you may have an outline typed at the beginning of your document, followed by many pages of content. The first thing I would recommend is separating your pages according to your outline. Paging and formatting will be a little different for a print format vs. an eBook. First, I will discuss the formatting of the interior for a print version of a book.

I highly recommend considering multiple formats for your book. Some readers prefer to save paper and read eBooks, while others prefer to hold a book in their hand, so it's a good idea to give readers both formatting options.

If you are setting up your book for both print format and eBook, you will need separate files for uploading during the self-publishing process. The interior is almost the same, with a couple exceptions:

- You may or may not need page numbers for your eBook. If your book is all text or mostly text, then it can be setup with a reflowable text option and pages will automatically adjust depending on the digital device used to read your book. In this case, you will not need page numbers. On the other hand, if your book is image heavy, you can opt for a fixed layout option which keeps each page intact when it is viewed as an eBook. I'll discuss more about this in Step 6. The Self Publishing Process.
- If you have blank pages to separate sections or chapters for the printed version of your manuscript, you won't need to include those blank pages for your eBook.

Before I explain the process that I use to format the interior of my books, I want to mention that KDP does offer paperback manuscript templates which have the page size and margins setup for you. I included a link for this in the Resources section in the back of this book. I don't use the templates for interior content since I setup my own formatting, but you can check out those templates to get started if you like.

To help you keep track of your formatting settings, refer to the Formatting Worksheet in the companion workbook.

Trim Size

By now, I hope you have been combing through lots of books to get ideas, whether online or in bookstores. The trim size of a book is basically the dimensions for the book. The most popular trim sizes are 5" X 8", 5.5" X 8.5" and 6" X 9". Sometimes it's hard to imagine the dimensions without seeing them. When I first started writing and self-publishing, I measured a variety of books around the house to compare trim sizes, which helped me decide on the best trim size for my books. Initially, I selected 6" X 9" for my first series, but because my software training books were image heavy, I needed more room for images. So, I decided to use 7" X 10". For my PowerPoint book, I also created a Large Print version with a trim size of 8" X 10", which is one of my bestsellers. For my children's rhyming books, I went with a square size of 8 ½" X 8 ½". Once you decide on a trim size, you'll need to setup the page layout in your software program. In Microsoft Word, in the Layout tab, select Size, More Paper Sizes, then enter the corresponding dimensions for the Width and Height fields. Make sure the Apply to option is set to Whole Document, then click OK.

Note: If you decide to use a paperback manuscript template from KDP, the page size is already setup for you.

Margins

For margins, .75" or 1" inch margins work well with many books, but it depends on your trim size and the number of pages. If your book is a smaller trim size, you may want to have narrower margins to allow a little more space per page for text and other content.

In Microsoft Word, to select margin settings, in the Layout tab, select Margins. Standard margins will display, but I recommend selecting Custom Margins to view all margin settings. Next, the Page Layout dialog box displays. In the Margin tab, make any changes to the Top, Bottom, Left and Right Margins. Make sure the Apply to option at the bottom is set to Whole Document, then click OK.

Note: If you decide to use a paperback manuscript template from KDP, margins are already setup for you.

Fonts and Text Attributes

- For nonfiction, I like to use a sans serif font like Calibri or Arial. Sans serif fonts are the plainer fonts without the serif, which is the little line or stroke along the edges of the font. The reason they are called "sans" serif fonts is because the French word "sans," means "without." Sans serif typefaces are considered more modern than serif typefaces and they often used in nonfiction books. Common font sizes are between 10 and 12 pt., and might be as much as 14 or 16 pt. for Large Print books. For my technology books, I used Calibri 11 pt. but for my Large Print PowerPoint book I used Arial 16 pt. For this book which you are reading, I'm using Calibri 12 pt. Chapter headings would typically be 14 to 16 pt.
- Fonts for children's books are typically more decorative and eye-catching, so this varies depending on the overall theme of the book.
- Fiction books, especially romance and literary fiction books usually have classic fonts. Serif fonts are often used. Serif fonts help with readability, and are generally easier on the reader's eye when reading because the stroke of the serif font leads the reader's eye from one letter to the next. Common font size ranges from 10 to 12. Chapter headings would typically be larger, ranging from 14 to 16 pt.

No matter what font size you select, the most important thing is to make sure content is clear and legible for the reader.

For text attributes, I bold all my headings. I use italics for emphasis and for special statement like quotes or captions. When applying text attributes, consider using the Format Painter to duplicate formatting from one area of a document to another. For a demonstration on how to use the Format Painter, go to my channel, www.youtube.com/user/easylearningweb and search using the hashtag *#ezword12* (be sure to use the inner search box within my channel instead of the search bar at the first top, which will search all of YouTube).

To apply text attributes to all body text, you can modify the style called Normal. In the Styles group on the Home tab, right click on Normal and click Modify. On the Modify Style dialog box, click Font on the bottom left and make any necessary changes and click Ok to save your changes. This is a handy and quick way to make global changes in a snap.

Layout of Pages for Print Version (Paperback or Hardcover)

I have included a list below to demonstrate how I typically setup the pages of a print book (paperback or hardcover). There will be some variations depending on genre. One thing to keep in mind for print versions of a book is where the pages will be positioned – either on the left, or the right. Remember that odd numbered pages will be on the right for the reader, and even numbered pages will appear on the left. Also remember that even pages are on the under side of pages; therefore, the first page of each chapter, along with the beginning of important sections should begin on an odd numbered page.

Sample Layout of Pages (Print Version)

Page #	Page Description	Setup Notes
1	Inside cover page	This can be text including the title and author, and/or an image. In some cases, I like to use a reduced version size or cropped image of the front book cover.
2	Copyright page	Information and formatting for a copyright page varies, but at a minimum you want to include the copyright statement, a disclaimer about copyright protection, and the ISBN #.
3	Dedication	This is of course optional and depends on the type of book and genre.
4	Blank page	
5	Foreword	Optional; an introduction of the book written by someone other than the author.
6	Foreword, continued, or a blank page	
7,8	About This Book (or How to Use This Book)	Optional; explains the contents of the book or how to use the book (nonfiction books).
9	Free Gift	Optional; for all types of books; can be a free PDF offer like a free chapter of book 2, a recipe, a related guide, etc. Great for building your email list.
10	Blank page	
11	Introduction	Optional and depends on the genre; this can used in place of About This Book.
12	Blank page	

Page #	Page Description	Setup Notes
13 -on	Chapter 1, 2, 3, etc…. (or Parts or Sections)	Start each new chapter on an odd numbered page. For children's picture books, chapters or sections are generally not used; illustrated pages would typically begin on an odd numbered page.
Odd #	Resources, Bibliography or Appendix	Depending on the type of book, you may need to include resources, citations, or appendices in the back of the book.
Odd # or Even #	Thank You/Review Request	Thank you message to readers and a place to ask them for a book review.
Odd #	Other Books by [Author] or About the Author	Add thumbnail images of other book in the series, or other books/publications. You can also use this page to include additional author information and social media links.

Using Page Breaks

The use of hard page breaks allows you to control when the current page ends, and a new page begins. This is especially important for fixed layout books where you want to keep text and images together on the same page, or for children's books or other books which are created with image files. If your book is all or mostly text, you can just let your software start a new page automatically via soft page breaks. The use of hard page breaks depends on the type of content in your book and the type of format your book will be published in (print version, eBook, etc.).

In Microsoft Word, hard page breaks can be inserted by pressing *Ctrl + Enter*, or by selecting *Page Break* from the *Insert* tab in the Ribbon. You can even go a step further in Word and insert section breaks and start the new section on either the next even-numbered page or the next odd-numbered page. These options are available in the Breaks drop-down menu in the Layout tab.

As a rule of thumb, when you want to start content on a brand-new page or to insert a blank page, insert a hard page break. Otherwise, just keep typing and a new page will automatically be added when you have reached the bottom margin on the current page.

Creating an Interactive Table of Contents

The outline you originally created in Step. 2 can serve as a table of contents. However, in the long run, you may want to consider converting your outline into an interactive table of contents. I like to do this as I finalize my content, so I can update my Table of Contents and instantly see the results. You can accomplish this in one of two ways: using heading styles or using bookmarks.

Option #1: Automatic TOC Using Heading Styles

Word has built in Heading Styles which can be found in the Styles group of the *Home* tab in the Ribbon. To apply a heading style, just select your text, then click on *Heading 1*, *Heading 2*, or *Heading 3* to apply the style. Then when you are ready to generate your table of contents, from the *References* tab in the ribbon, click *Table of Contents* and select one of the TOC styles to automatically insert it in your document. When your content changes, to update your TOC, just click on the top of the TOC, and select *Update Table*; then select *Update Entire Table*. You can also click *Update Table* from the *References* tab.

There's one caveat to using this method. For one reason or another, even though the table of contents is clickable in Word, and clickable when you convert it to a PDF, they don't always work when you convert your file for publishing to an eBook. Therefore, you can use bookmarks as an alternative option. For help on bookmarks, see **Option #2: Manual TOC Setup Using Heading Styles and Bookmarks**, on the next page.

If you do use Heading styles to build your TOC as you go, it's easy to generate and update your table of contents periodically so you can see how your manuscript is shaping up.

If you need help setting up your table of contents using Heading styles, go to www.youtube.com/user/easylearningweb and search using the hashtag **#ezword14** (*be sure to use the <u>inner search box</u> within my channel instead of the search bar at the first top, which will search all of YouTube*).

Option #2: Manual TOC Setup Using Heading Styles and Bookmarks

To setup the electronic links for your table of contents using bookmarks, first, make sure you have your outline text on a separate page in your document, preferably after the copyright page. For example:

Foreword
About This Book
Free Gift
Chapter 1
Chapter 2
Chapter 3
Chapter 4
Chapter 5
Thank you
Other Books

Make sure that each of these titles (on the corresponding pages throughout your manuscript) are formatted with a Heading style. Next, for each of the titles in your outline, do the following:

1. Select the text (for example, select "Foreword")
2. From the *Insert* tab, select *Link* (or right click and select Link)
3. Make sure *Place in this Document* is selected from the *Insert Hyperlink* dialog box.
4. Each title (word or phrase) for your outline should be listed under Headings. Scroll down if needed; then select the title (in this example, select "Foreword") under *Headings*.
5. Click *OK*.
6. The text is then hyperlinked to the corresponding page in your book.
7. Repeat steps 1. Through 6. for each title in your outline to build the links for your TOC.

If you want to add other items to your outline for text which is not formatted with Heading Styles, you can do so with Bookmarks.

Should You Create a Style Guide?

If you are creating a book series, a style guide is a helpful asset because it will help you keep track of all formatting styles and preferences. A style guide is essential to ensure that all books, publications, reports, lessons, etc. are consistent with regards to formatting, color scheme, style, and theme. For some genres, a list of standard terminology and acronyms may also be helpful. The latter would be more common for nonfiction.

Do you need more help with Microsoft Word? My very first self-published book is a collection of 35 mini-lessons on – you guessed it, Microsoft Word! Earlier in this book, you may remember me mentioning that my first book was part of a Microsoft Office How-To series of books and videos. I learned a long, long time ago that everyone learns differently so I like to offer different formats for learning. In addition to my Microsoft Word Tips, Tricks and Shortcuts book, I have companion videos available on my YouTube channel. You can find the Microsoft Word playlist by visiting my channel, www.youtube.com/user/easylearningweb then click Playlists, and select the Microsoft Word How-To Videos playlist.

Do you have a formatting question?

If you have a formatting question, you can submit a question by using the *Contact Us* form on my blog. Go to www.ameliaswritingcorner.com and then select *Contact Us* from the menu.

The Editing Process

Editing and Proofing – Do it Yourself or Hire Someone?

So, you have a draft of your manuscript ready, and you think it's perfect. However, unless you are a professional editor, a second pair of eyes is almost essential.

Should you proof it yourself or hire someone? How much does editing cost? Is editing the same as proofreading?

First, be sure to obtain a few quotes from different editors. You can post a question in author groups on social media such as Facebook groups, or LinkedIn groups.

There is definitely a difference between editing and proofreading.

Editing or Line Editing – This may include checking that the tone is consistent throughout your writing, that content is organized, and that there is proper use of vocabulary.

Copyediting/Proofreading – This may include checking for grammar/spelling errors, typographical errors, and punctuation errors. It may also include a final proofing to make sure it is 100% ready to roll.

Also, you'll want to ask potential editors how many passes of your manuscript they will make as well. Some editors will edit and/or proof up to three times or passes of your manuscript. As far as pricing, this seems to vary a lot and depends on the type of editing, the genre, and the word count.

For my first series, since I had been writing and editing lots of technical training materials over the years, and, since my books were nonfiction, computer how-to themed, I felt I didn't need any heavy-duty sentence restructuring or line editing. However, after hearing how important it was to make sure a manuscript is 100% polished and ready, I decided to hire someone just for proofing. Was it worth it? Yes and no. Yes, for peace of mind; and, no because I discovered a double "the" on one of the pages after go live, which I quickly corrected.

For my children's rhyming stories, at the time, I was a member of a local chapter writing critique group through SCBWI, so I would bring my children's stories to the group for critiquing. The other members of the group helped me with the rhythm of the rhyming. They also helped me with sentence structure and grammar. That is one suggestion on how to collaborate with other writers for feedback. I also proofed my stories many times but after ordering a proof, I found a typographical error. It never hurts to have some fine-tune editing done to make sure your book is 100% error free. Also, it is extremely important to order a proof copy of your printed book and review it again to make sure everything is correct. I discuss more about ordering proof copies in Step. 6, The Publishing Process.

Even when you hire an editor, there are no guarantees. If you are writing rhyming children's stories, it helps to do some research about how to structure your phrases. With rhyming, the rules are not the same. Punctuation in rhyming is used to guide the reader to pause, to help with the rhythm of the rhyming, and each phrase may not necessarily be a complete sentence. Therefore, if you hire an editor, make sure the editor is familiar with how rhyming can be structured differently.

With any genre, when hiring an editor or proofreader, make sure the person has experience with your type of book and genre. Ask for examples and testimonials. In some cases, you could consider having someone edit or proof a small sampling of your book to see if it is a good fit.

Spelling and Grammar Check

Most word processors have a spelling and grammar check. Otherwise, you might have to use a separate app. In the latest version of Microsoft Word, the Spelling and Grammar check is now combined under the *Editor* function in the *Review* tab. The *Editor* provides spelling, grammar and writing suggestions. I would suggest running the *Editor* several times. When you make changes to your manuscript, and for each draft, run the *Editor* again to double-check spelling and grammar. This is just *one* tool you can use to check your content and apply edits.

I also use the Grammarly app as well. There is a free version which checks for misspelled words, imperfect grammar, and punctuation mistakes. The premium version offers 400 types of features, and checks for grammatical errors, provides vocabulary enhancement suggestions, detects plagiarism, and provides citation suggestions.

Another tool to consider using to help you with your writing is ProWritingAid, which is more focused on writing style and readability. In addition to checking spelling and grammar, it also looks at how a sentence is constructed to make sure the structure, style, and tense are correct. ProWritingAid has a 14-day money back guarantee, so you can try it out and contact them within 2 weeks if you want to cancel. There is also a ProWritingAid Add-in for Microsoft Word, Open Office, Scrivener, GoogleDocs and various browsers including Chrome. The Add-in offers a free trial and then you can decide if you want to purchase.

Final Proofing and Read Out Loud Tools

Whether you decide to hire someone for line editing or just proofing, I would recommend doing one final proofing yourself, by reading your whole book out loud. You can either read it yourself, or have your computer read to you. I like to use the *Read Aloud* feature in Microsoft Word. From the *Review* tab, just click *Read Aloud* in the *Speech* group. This opens a pane on the side of your document which allows you to *Play* and *Pause*, jump to the *Previous* or *Next* paragraph, or access *Settings*. In *Settings*, you can change the voice speed as well as select from a variety of voices.

There are also lots of other apps you can use on your computer which can read your text aloud.

If you're following along using the companion workbook, use the Editing Tracking Worksheets on pages 51 through 55, to track your editing progress including spelling, grammar and sentence structure. Recording the completion for each round of editing gets you one step closer to finalizing your manuscript!

Your Book Cover

Your book cover and title are two of the most important aspects of your book. An attractive, high-quality cover and well-formatted interior can help drive readers to your book.

What Do Readers Look For? Readers like to see similar styles when considering books in the same genres. In Step 3., you completed exercises to search for bestselling books in your genre. Now is a good time to refer back to your list, taking note of what you liked or didn't like on the front cover, and any similarities you noticed.

Here are some book cover suggestions for different genres:

- **Romance Novel book covers** – Use photographic images to portray your characters in a loving embrace; for historical fiction romance, use fashion and color to represent the corresponding era or time in history .
- **Science Fiction book covers** - Use fonts and illustrations to evoke imagination.
- **Health and Wellness book covers** - Use soothing tones and photographic imagery to create personal connections.
- **Non-Fiction book covers** – Use modern, trending graphics and elements which support the theme of your book.
- **Children's Books** – Use colorful, fun images; include characters from your book presented in a unique way to make the cover pop.

Book Cover Images

Images on the book cover, including the front, spine and back, as well as interior images should all be high-resolution, or at least 300 DPI. Be careful not to solely use free images you find on the internet. Not only may they be copyrighted images, but they may also be common photos or images which someone else may use on their book cover. The best thing to do is use a variety of graphics to create something unique. If you have no experience with graphics or design, then it may be best to hire a professional cover designer to ensure your cover is the best it could be. No matter what you may have heard, many readers do judge a book by it's cover.

DIY vs. Hiring a Professional Book Cover Designer

It's important to do your research when considering what type of cover you would like for your book. Here's a list of what I did to research and learn about book covers, and some dos and don'ts:

Do's:

- Browse on Amazon.com and other websites and look at book covers for similar books in your genre.
- Look on pixabay.com for ideas and download images and backgrounds that you like. However, I wouldn't necessarily recommend using free images directly from websites such as pixabay.com. Instead, whether you are designing your own book cover or hiring a designer, it's ok to incorporate some images providing you make it unique and attractive. In other words, make it your own and don't just use stock photos.
- Consider having 3 colors:2 main contrasting colors and 1 accent color.
- Watch how-to create book covers on YouTube. One person to look for is Derek Murphy. I learned a lot from his videos about what to do or not do if you are designing your own book covers.
- Post mockup images of your proposed book covers on author groups on Facebook and ask people to vote for their favorite book cover.
- Reach out to professional graphic artists for professional opinions, as well as pricing on book cover designs. Remember to inquire to determine how many rounds of edits are included in the price.

Don'ts:

- Don't recreate the wheel and try to create something totally different as compared to similar books in your genre. The trick is to make it similar to other books in the same genre, but with a unique twist to make it better.
- Don't try to create your own book cover if you have no graphic experience.
- If you hire a designer, don't limit yourself to just one; it may be helpful to hire two designers initially until you find the best match. The same is true for illustrators. Shop around and look at sample images and designs to make sure it's a good fit.

Book Cover Creation Tools and Process

- Here are different scenarios I tried when creating book covers:
    - For my technology book series, I created the front covers after doing extensive research for similar books in the genre. I reached out to 3 professional graphic artists to ask them their professional opinion. This is important, especially if it's the first time you are designing your own covers.
    - For my children's book series, my illustrator designed the front cover image but I purchased the source file in case I wanted to make any changes at a later date. I designed the back cover layout. These books were too thin to have spine text.
    - For my Author Journey Success series, I hired a professional designer and they designed and laid out the front cover, spine and back cover for each book in the series.
- For the book covers that I did design, I used Canva Pro. This includes laying out the front, spine and back cover images. There is a free version, but I recommend the Pro version to get access to all the features and graphics. For more help with Canva, go to my YouTube channel, https://www.youtube.com/user/easylearningweb, click Playlists, then select the Canva playlist.
- I used the KDP template in conjunction with Canva to layout the full cover design. The URL to download book cover templates which contains instructions is: https://kdp.amazon.com/en_US/cover-templates. You will need 3 pieces of information including your trim size, page count and paper color. Once the template is downloaded, it's important to follow the instructions on how to layout your book cover images using the template. You can contact KDP support for assistance or refer to their help screens for more information.
- For the hard cover versions of my children's book, I used IngramSpark. The cover size was slightly different, so I also downloaded a template from IngramSpark to use in conjunction with Canva for my book cover. See the Resources section in the back of this book for more information.

Your Book Title

If your book is nonfiction, your title should be keyword friendly and catchy. Depending on the genre, it should follow along with other successful books on the same topic. In other words, if your book is about Skydiving, look at other books on the same topic to get ideas.

If your book is fiction, your title should still be catchy, but it wouldn't have the same keyword friendly title as a nonfiction book.

In Step 3., as part of the research process, you learned about several tools to use for keyword research, including the Amazon and Google search agents, Keyword Tool, Kindle Spy, Publisher Rocket, and KWFinder. Visit these tools again if needed to refine your book title.

After you decide on a book title, consider creating several mockup book covers with possible titles which you can post online on author groups for feedback. You can also create a online poll or survey as well. After I created mockup cover designs for my books, I posted 3 designs on several different author groups on Facebook. I received a lot of helpful feedback on both the cover design as well as the title. After I reworked the title, I posted three redesigns on a second poll, on three different Facebook author groups. Sharing your mockup design and redesigns on author groups is not only helpful for feedback, but it is also another example of author networking and collaboration.

Important Note About Your Book Cover and Book Title

A few months after I launched my first book, which was a book of tips, tricks, and shortcuts for Microsoft Word, I decided to change one of the colors used on the book cover. I thought the blue color I selected looked washed out and decided I wanted to use a darker blue color to better contrast with the yellow color. In addition, I wanted to change some wording in the book title. I then learned a valuable lesson: You can change the book cover as many times as needed, providing that the title remains the same. As far as changing any text in your title, that is not doable. Once your book is live, there is certain information you cannot change including the title, author, publisher, and publication date. The only way to have a different title is to create a new book listing. In my case, I had no choice. I had a correction to make in the title and I decided to create a new book listing. I figured, no problem, I'll just delete the old book listing. Then I learned another valuable lesson: once you create a book listing on Amazon, it is there FOREVER! You can unpublish it if you like, which will make it appear as "unavailable". I decided I didn't want any of my books to say "unavailable", so I kept the old listing as is with one exception: at the top of the book description, I put a large note in capital letters which read:

PLEASE NOTE: THIS IS THE ORIGINAL VERSION; THERE IS A NEW AND IMPROVED 2ND EDITION NOW AVAILABLE FOR THIS BOOK (Kindle and Paperback Versions Available - See www.amazon.com/author/ameliagriggs for the newer edition).

So, in summary, make sure your book title and subtitle are perfectly ready for when you move to the next step, which is the publishing process.

Congratulations!

You have now reached the 5th milestone in your journey!

6

The Self-Publishing Process

Step 6: The Publishing Process

Publishing Options

At this point in your journey, you should have your formatted manuscript, along with your book title and book cover, ready for the presses! But first – the big decision: how should you publish your book? There are basically three options when it comes to publishing your book:

- **Traditional Publishing** – With traditional publishing, you would typically need to have a literary agent who works with the large traditional publishers to get your book published. To get a literary agent, you would need to write query letters, pitching your book idea for consideration. With traditional publishers, you don't have full creative control, as they will make some of the decisions about your book. For example, for children's books, they may use their own illustrator which may or may not be to your liking. As far as marketing, you still have to market your book, although they will help with book signings, etc.
- **Vanity Publishing** – This is not the same as traditional publishing. Anytime a publishing company offers to publish your book and they charge a fee (usually a hefty fee), they are a vanity publisher. The services which a vanity publisher charges you depends on the type of package you purchase. Before you consider a vanity publishing company, it's important to look at their reputation, their reviews and testimonials, and the types of books they have published, including the genre, the design, and the quality. Vanity publishers may also charge you a fee in addition to taking a percentage of your royalty. They might also require you to purchase a minimum number of printed books.
- **Self-Publishing** – With self-publishing, you are publishing your own book, and you have full creative rights, so you will be making all the decisions about your book. You can decide if you want to do it all yourself, or if you want to outsource some parts of the process. You can find an editor you like, an illustrator you prefer and a cover designer who has artwork that you love.

If you're not sure what type of publishing is right for you, ask yourself the following questions:

How soon do you want to publish? If you want to publish as soon as possible, then rule out traditional publishing which can take many years. I know several authors who have written beautiful manuscripts but have been holding out for many years waiting for a literary agent to reply to their query letters. I'm not sure what the timeline is for vanity publishing, but if you fork over your wallet, I'm sure they can accommodate your schedule. The good news is that you can publish as soon as possible if you self-publish, and I can tell you how to do it for free, or almost for free: publishing an eBook means there is no cost whatsoever for book printing, so this is one option. However, in the long run, I am going to recommend that you consider both eBook and paperback at the very least.

How big or small is your budget? Even if you have a budget of $5,000, or even $1,000, why should you pay a vanity publisher who will most likely overcharge you for something that you can do yourself? The amount of money you would pay a vanity publishing company can be better spent by hiring a trustworthy editor, an illustrator (for children's books) or book cover designer and running ads for marketing.

Are you a well-known celebrity or public figure? Many of us are not, but if you are fortunate enough to have a million followers and well-know, then traditional publishers may be knocking on your door.

Why Self-Publishing?

I think you know where this is going. Even if you want to try to get a book deal some day with a traditional publishing company, while you are waiting in the winds, why not try self-publishing? As you know, I self-published my own books, so I didn't use a publishing company. To self-publish, I use Amazon's KDP (Kindle Direct Publishing) which is a free tool used to setup your book title, and upload your book files, including your interior manuscript and your exterior book cover. For the hard cover versions of my children's books, I used Ingram Spark, since Amazon's KDP does not have a hard cover option at this time.

Putting It All Together with KDP

Although there are other companies to consider for your book, to get started, I would recommend using KDP (Kindle Direct Publishing) which is a free option and is an excellent starting point for beginners. You can always expand from there later.

If you are interested in hard cover, KDP offers a hard cover option, but only for books with a minimum of 75 pages. In addition to my paperback and eBook formats, I wanted to offer hard cover for my children's books, so I decided to use IngramSpark. IngramSpark is not free and charges $49.00 for a new book listing. Once you upload your book files, if you make any edits, they charge an additional $25.00 per upload. Sometimes there is a coupon code offer which waives one or both of these fees. I created a video comparing the quality of KDP and Ingram Spark printing which can be found on my YouTube channel. Visit www.youtube.com/user/easylearningweb and go to the Self-Publishing playlist.

Let's Talk About Kindle Direct Publishing

Amazon is one of the biggest platforms in the world, and they make it easy and simple to self-publish with the free KDP tool. So, when I first started, I didn't think twice about where I wanted to upload my books.

I'm not saying this is the one and only way to begin your self-publishing uploading process, but it's how I got started and it's an easy, free method for *you* to consider. It's like a no brainer for newbies who want to self-publish quickly. Yes, there are lots of other platforms you can use and other companies who will do the work for you, but that costs money. If you're not sure where to begin, my recommendation is to try the KDP process. You have nothing to lose, since KDP is free. For additional costs for a cover design, illustrations, and marketing, you have control on how much you spend based on your budget. If you are wondering what to do about marketing, there's a list of book promotion ideas to get you started in Step 7. in this book. There's also another book in the Author Journey Success series to help you with marketing and book promotion.

Preparing Your Manuscript for Print Versions vs. eBook Format

Paperback

Paperback or other print formats should or could include the following features:

- Page numbers (exceptions are children's picture books, and zero or low-content books such as blank journals, etc.)
- Headers and Footers

For your paperback manuscript file, you will need to prepare a file to upload on KDP for the interior content for your book. If your book has images or elements that bleed to the edges of your pages, such as children's books, image-heavy cookbooks, etc. you must upload your manuscript as a PDF. If your book does not contain bleed, you can upload your manuscript as a PDF, DOC, DOCX, RTF, HTML, or TXT file. KDP will then automatically convert these file types to PDF. Personally, I like to save my Word document to PDF to make it easier. In Word, just click File, Save As and select PDF for the Save As Type field in the Save As dialog box; then click OK. Once your file is saved as a PDF, it's a good idea to review the file in Adobe Reader to check the layout of all pages.

eBook

eBook formats do not have to include:

- Page numbers (this is true for most eBooks if you use the reflowable text option; however, there are exceptions such as image-heavy books with text that should remain with the image, or other types of books where you want each page to remain static; in this case, if your pages are to remain static, you may want to include page numbers, which was the case for the eBook versions of all my technology books)
- Headers and Footers
- Excess blank pages

For your eBook manuscript file, there are a variety of file formats you can use when uploading your file. Before discussing file formats for eBooks, let's review the different layout options.

Fixed Layout Format vs. Reflowable File Format (eBooks)

To prepare your eBook, once the content is 100% proofed and ready to go, make a copy of your manuscript file and rename it something suitable for your eBook version. There are two options to consider for the layout of your eBook:

- **Fixed Layout Format** – This option keeps your pages in a fixed layout when viewing on an eBook. Pages are displayed the same way they will appear once printed, including the positioning of images, words, paragraphs, and columns. Examples of when fixed layout format is used include children's books, travel guides, photography books, art books, comic books, and image heavy instructional books. With fixed layout format, since each page remains static, any headers, footers, page numbers, etc. will remain intact on each page.
- **Reflowable File Format** – This format is designed to be displayed on a variety of screen sizes. The content on each page changes depending on the device. HTML and plain text are examples of "reflowable" formats. Reflowable file format is the best option for books that contain mostly text content and have a relatively straightforward layout. The content will "reflow" based on the reading device or software being used and may change appearance depending on the personal settings of the reader. Examples of when reflowable file format is used include novels, fiction, and non-fiction books with all or mostly text.

If your eBook will use reflowable file format, then remove the page numbering, headers and footers, and any other page dependent embellishments (such as images or logos you have incorporated at the top or bottom of pages) from your document. For both fixed layout format and reflowable file format, you will also want to remove any blank pages which aren't needed as well.

To prepare your eBook file to upload on KDP, you need to convert your manuscript to one of the following file formats: DOCX, KCP, HTML, MOBI, ePUB, RTF, TXT or PDF, all of which are explained on the next page. The list can be overwhelming, and although I want to explain all the file options for you, I want to tell you upfront that there's an easy method I use to convert a file using the free tool, Kindle Create, which is available to download for free. First, I will review the file type options, and then I will explain how to use Kindle Create.

File Format Options For Uploading an eBook on KDP

- **Microsoft Word (DOC/DOCX)** – Although I created my manuscripts in Word, I didn't upload Word files because files with complex formatting might not convert as well, and I needed my content formatting to stay put, in the fixed layout format. If your manuscript is extremely straightforward and contains all text, and you are using the reflowable file format option, a DOCX file may be suitable for uploading.

- **Kindle Create (KPF)** – I used this format for my first three books, which were computer themed. Originally, I used the free tool called Kindle Textbook Creator, but this is now part of Kindle Create. With this free tool, you have the option of creating a reflowable or Print Replica Kindle Package Format (KPF) file. The reflowable option resizes text so that pages adjust automatically on all Kindle devices and free Kindle reading applications. The Replica Kindle Package Format maintains the look of your PDF file (and your final print edition), but it does not resize text automatically on Kindle devices. This option works well if you have image-heavy books where you don't want the page layout to change. I needed this option for my computer-themed books in order to keep images and text together on corresponding pages.

- **HTML (ZIP, HTM, or HTML)** – This option is best for HTML specific manuscripts. In this case, you will need to compress your HTML file(s) to a zip file in order to upload it on KDP. If you don't have images in your manuscript, you can upload your HTML file without compressing it to a ZIP file.

- **MOBI** – MOBI is the name given to the format developed for the MobiPocket Reader. MOBI is a reflowable file format, and doesn't allow fixed layout. To convert your manuscript to MOBI format requires that you use a third-party tool such as Calibre.

- **ePub** – ePub is a format which can be downloaded and read on devices like smartphones, tablets, computers, or e-readers. It is a technical standard published by the International Digital Publishing Forum (IDPF). To convert your manuscript to MOBI format requires that you use a third-party tool.

- **Rich Text Format (RTF)** – Most text editors allow you to save to Rich Text Format (RTF). Formatting is very limited with this type of file.

- **Plain Text (TXT)** – Plain text editors like Notepad allow you to save to Plain Text (TXT). This format doesn't allow images, and has very limited formatting capabilities.
- **Adobe PDF** – PDF format stands for Portable Document Format. It may not convert well if your manuscript contains embedded formatting or images.

If you do decide to convert to either MOBI or ePub format using Calibre, you can email either file to yourself and then open the file on your mobile device for testing purposes to see if it looks ok before you upload it on KDP.

It is also recommended that you review and validate your file with Kindle Previewer before you upload your book to KDP. Kindle Previewer is covered later in this chapter.

Kindle Create

Kindle Create is a free, easy-to-use tool that you can use to convert your file for uploading your eBook on KDP. See the Resources section at the end of the book for the download link.

Once you have downloaded Kindle Create, launch the app. Use the following steps to convert your file. Note: You can use Kindle Create for both fixed layout format and reflowable file format.

1. Select: ⊕ *Create New* on the upper right and click *Choose* on the bottom right. As an alternative, from the *File* menu, you can select *New Project*.
2. For the next step, choose one of the following:
    a. Reflowable – for text based manuscript from a Word file (this option will allow the reader to change the size of the fonts, margins and other properties on their reading device).
    b. Comics – for manuscripts consisting of a series of JPG files or PDF.
    c. Print Replica – for fixed layout formatted manuscript from a PDF file.
3. Select *Choose File*.
4. From the *Import From File* dialog box, select your file and click *Open*.
5. Depending on the layout option you selected in step 2. above, the import process may take a few minutes.

6. Next, do one of the following:
   a. If you selected the *Reflowable* option for a text-based manuscript, a message will appear when the import is complete; click *Continue* to proceed. Kindle Create will then automatically find and apply chapter title elements in your book; click *Get Started*. Make sure the chapters that Kindle Create found are correct; uncheck any which are not correct. When finished, click *Accept Selected*.
   b. If you selected the *Comics* option (for children's picture books, for example), you will be prompted to select book properties before your selecting your JPG or PDF file(s) to import. A message will appear when the import is complete; click *Continue* to proceed.
   c. If you selected the *Print Replica* option, if you have any hyperlinks in your file, you will be prompted to preserve your links; click *Yes* to ensure your hyperlinks are embedded and preserved in your eBook.
7. Periodically, you may be prompted to save your file. Be sure to click *Yes, Save*, enter a name for your file, and click *Save*.
8. The pages of your manuscript will be displayed as thumbnails on the left. The selected page displays in the center pane. Take a few moments to click through all your pages to preview your manuscript.
9. Next, to see how your book will look to readers on different devices, click Preview on the upper right. You can change the device and other options as needed. When finished, close the Preview window by clicking on the X on the upper right.
10. If you need more help, explore the *Help* menu where you can find additional information as well as a Kindle Create Tutorial.
11. When you're happy with the pages of your eBook, the final step is to export your file. Click the *Generate* button in the upper right-hand corner. This creates a publishable file (in KPF format) that can be uploaded to KDP. In the *Save File for Publication* dialog box, enter a name for your file, and click *Save*.
12. Take note of where the exported (KPF file) is saved because this is the file you will need to upload for your eBook.

You are almost ready to upload your files for your eBook and/or paperback!

Refer to Publishing Checklist in the companion workbook to make sure you have everything you need to publish your book!

In addition to your manuscript file(s) which you prepared in the previous step, you will also need the information below on hand to enter during the upload process. I would recommend typing the values for all the fields below in a Notepad file; then you can just copy and paste the information on KDP during the upload process. *See the Information Checklist in the Publishing Process Tracking section in the companion workbook to track your information.*

- Book Title and Subtitle
- Series Information - if your book will be part of a series.
- Edition Number - leave blank; this is for new editions of an existing book.
- Author name
- Contributor names - other authors, illustrators, etc.
- Description - this is the description which will be listed on Amazon directly under your book's thumbnail.
- Keywords - prepare 7 search-friendly keywords or keyword phrases; if you need help, refer to the tools for Keywords in Step 3. in this book.
- Categories - refer to the category research in Step 3. and use the categories you prepared in Exercise 3c.
- Age and Grade Range - only applies to children's book.
- Trim Size - dimensions of your book.
- Paperback Cover Finish - decide ahead of time if you want matte or glossy; to help you decide: the Matte finish has minimal sheen and is more common for novels and other fiction, whereas the Glossy finish is shiny and is more common for textbooks, children's book and non-fiction books.
- Pricing - Now is the time to do some research for pricing; it's important to price your book right so it's not too high or not too low.

Reminders: During the upload process for your eBook, you will also need your front cover image (JPG file), and for your paperback upload, you will need your full cover image including the front, spine and back.

Kindle Previewer

Before uploading your eBook on KDP, you can optionally download another app called the Kindle Previewer. If you decide not to use Kindle Create to prepare and convert your manuscript for uploading (which has it's own Previewer), you may want to consider downloading and using the Kindle Previewer as an additional way to preview your book.

The Kindle Previewer is a free desktop application that enables you to preview how your books will appear when delivered to customers. You can preview your book in different screen sizes, display orientations and font sizes.

To understand everything about book format for Kindle and for download links for the Kindle Previewer, visit the following link:
https://www.amazon.com/gp/feature.html/?docId=1000765261

It is also recommended that you download the Kindle app on your computer as well as your mobile device. The Kindle Desktop for PC (or MAC) is free. Follow the link for "Kindle for PC [Download]", and click "MAC Download" or "PC Download" on this link:
https://www.amazon.com/Amazon-Digital-Services-LLC-Download/dp/B00UB76290

On your mobile devices, including your iPhone or Android phone, iPad or another tablet, you can search for and download the free Kindle App to preview your eBook on there as well.

Other Ways to Preview Your eBook and Paperback

In both the eBook and Paperback title setup, take advantage of the online preview option in KDP, which allows you to preview your book before publishing. This tool allows you to see what your book will look like after it's published (but before you put it live). You will see the online preview option during the upload processes which are covered in the next few pages.

For your paperback, I cannot emphasize enough how important it is to make sure you order a proof copy of your book, which you will see during the upload process. ***This should be done before you click the Publish button!***

Uploading Your Paperback Book on KDP

1. Go to kdp.amazon.com and login to KDP by clicking on *Sign in*. If this is the first time you are logging in to Kindle Directly Publishing, you can sign in with your Amazon account. If you don't have an Amazon account, click *Sign up* to setup your login and password.
2. After signing in, from the KDP dashboard, make sure the *Bookshelf* tab is selected at the top. Click *+ Create* and then select *Create Paperback*.
3. **Paperback Details tab**:
   a. **Language** – pick English or other language if needed.
   b. **Book Title and Subtitle** – Enter your search-friendly, catchy, title and subtitle here (try not to overstuff them with keywords).
   c. **Series** – Enter series name and number if this book is part of a series. Be sure to decide ahead of time if your book is part of a series. For example, for my first 3 books, I setup each book as part of a 3-book series. The name of my series is "Easy Learning Microsoft Office How-To Books". For each of my 3 books, I numbered each respectively as 1, 2 and 3.
   d. **Edition Number** – Enter a number here if this title is a new edition of an existing book.
   e. **Author** – Enter your own name, or alternate name if you are using a pen name.
   f. **Contributors** – Enter any additional authors who contributed to your book, or any other individuals like Illustrators or Translators.
   g. **Description** – Enter a detailed description of your book here. This could include your table of contents, benefits of your book, what you book has to offer, and what is different about your book. To make your description look nice, you can embed HTML codes in your description as well. Take a look at some descriptions of bestselling books to get an idea of what you might want your description to look like.
   h. **Publishing Rights** – Click the radio button to select your publishing rights. If you own your content, click the option for "I own the copyright...". The option for "This is a public domain work" is if you are using public domain content in your book. If you are using public domain content, you must make the content different in

some way, such as adding illustrations, translations or annotations.

    i. **Keywords** – Enter up to 7 keywords or keyword phrases that describe your book.

    j. **Categories** – Select up to 2 categories for your book. Refer back to the categories you selected during your pre-marketing research for Exercise 3c. in Step 3. Note: Once your book is published, you can add more categories by contacting KDP. It's a good idea to check the ranking in your categories periodically. In addition, check the categories in similar books to determine if it's time to change up some of your categories in an effect to improve the rankings. The categories should match up with the genre and topic of your book.

    k. **Large Print** – At the bottom of the Categories box, there is also an option for Large Print, which are for books that have a font size of 16 points or higher. If you check the "Large print" box, then the words "Large Print" will appear on your book's Amazon detail page. Checking the box won't change your book's font size.

    l. **Adult Content** – Providing your book does not contain any inappropriate languages, situations or images for children under the age of 18, select "No". Otherwise, if your book contains inappropriate content and you select "Yes", your book will not be included in general search results.

Click **Save and Continue** at this point to continue to the next tab.

4. **Paperback Content Tab:**

    a. **Print ISBN** – You can opt for a free KDP ISBN by clicking "Assign me a free KDP ISBN or purchase your own.

    Here's What I Did: For my first three books, I opted for the free KDP ISBN option since I decided to self-publish and sell on Amazon initially. This may be a good option if you're just starting out with self-publishing on KDP. For my other books, I purchased ISBNs from bowker.com

    More Info about the free KDP ISBNs: Your title will have 2 ISBNs. One is a 13-digit EAN (European Article Number) ISBN and the other is a 10-digit (International Standard Book Number) ISBN. The purpose of the ISBN is to establish your title with a publisher and specific edition and help retailers, libraries, and distributors search for your title.

If you decide to have your book distributed to other companies such as Ingram Spark, they cannot use an ISBN generated by KDP, so you would need to buy a full ISBN for the title transfer. Upon writing this book, the cost of purchasing one ISBN on bowker.com was $125, but you can purchase a pack of 10 for $295.00, which brings the price down to $29.50 per ISBN.

b. **Publication Date** – You can leave this blank the first time you publish your book, and the date will be filled in for you automatically.

c. **Print Options** – You can select Black and White interior with cream paper, Black and White interior with white paper, or Color interior with white paper. Romance and literary fiction books usually have cream colored interior for the pages, whereas non-fiction books normally have white interior page.

Here's What I Did: I opted for white paper, and for the interior, I experimented with both Black and White as well as Color. My lesson learned is that a book with color interior which is image-heavy (which describes my first 3 non-fiction books) is a lot more expensive to print, and you will need to set the price of your book higher as compared to a book with Black and White interior.

d. **Trim Size** – Select your book's trim size. By now, you should have the dimensions of your book selected, since you needed to select the size for your cover design.

e. **Bleed Settings** – Your book will only need the Bleed option if it contains elements such as images that extend to the edge of the page (for example, for children's books). Otherwise, select No Bleed.

f. **Paperback Cover Finish** – Select Matte or Glossy finish.

g. **Manuscript** – Click *Upload paperback manuscript* and select your file. PDF is the preferred format.

h. **Book Cover** – If for any reason, you don't have a book cover, you can try Cover Creator which allows you to make a book cover using your own image or KDP's stock image. In my opinion, it's better to have your full book cover created ahead of time. Click the *Upload a cover you already have* option and select your PDF file for your book cover.

i. **Book Preview** – Click *Launch Previewer* to preview your book. This may take a few minutes to load. In the Previewer, you can scroll through your pages to ensure that all pages look ok, and that nothing is cut off along the edges. If there are any issues, click *Exit Print Previewer*, and then return to your manuscript to make any corrections; resave as PDF and then return to step g. in this section to re-upload your manuscript. If everything looks fine in the Previewer, click *Approve* on the bottom right.

Click **Save and Continue** at this point to continue to the next tab.

5. **Paperback Rights and Pricing tab:**
   a. **Territories** – I usually pick All territories.
   b. **Primary Marketplace** – Choose the location where you expect the majority of your book sales.
   c. **Pricing, Royalty and Distribution** – In this section, you can enter different prices to calculate your royalty. Once you enter the list price you would like to sell your book for, the rate and royalty display. This is an estimate of how much you'll earn for each sale, based on the list price, royalty rate, and deducted print costs. On the far right, you can check the *Expanded Distribution* box to make your book available to bookstores and other distributors, reaching readers beyond Amazon. Large book distributors can make your title available to other online retailers, libraries, universities, and booksellers (beyond Amazon). This may be limited to certain marketplaces.

   Here's What I Did for Expanded Distribution: I have this option turned on for all my books. The only exception is for my hard cover books, which are self-published through IngramSpark. The

Expanded Distribution option on KDP is a good option to have your book pushed out to many additional retailers.

d. **Terms and Conditions** – Although it says to click publish to confirm that you agree with the terms and condition, ***DO NOT click the Publish Your Paperback Book button just yet!!!*** This will put your book live, which you don't want to do just yet. Instead, click *Save as Draft*. At this point, it's time to order a physical proof copy. The proof copy of your book will have a *Not for Resale* banner across the front and back of your book. The purpose of the proof copy is for you to double and triple check everything in your book, and your book cover. It's extremely important to proof your book before you put it live, to make sure everything is in order. To order proof copies:

1) Click the *Request printed proofs of this book* link which is located under the Terms and Conditions box.
2) Follow the instructions on the Request Proof Copies page to request one or more proof copies. Select your quantity and marketplace, and then click *Submit Proof Request*.
3) You will receive an email within a few hours with a link to complete your proof order. You must complete your purchase within 24 hours of receiving the email.
4) The proof takes about a week or so to arrive, but if you need it sooner, you can opt for faster shipping.

Finally, click *Save as Draft* to save your book listing in KDP.

Now that you have uploaded your book files for your paperback, while you are waiting for your proof to arrive in the mail, you can setup your eBook.

Uploading Your eBook on KDP

1. Go to kdp.amazon.com and login to KDP by clicking on *Sign in*. If this is the first time you are logging in to Kindle Directly Publishing, you can sign in with your Amazon account. If you don't have an Amazon account, click *Sign up* to setup your login and password.

2. After signing in, from the KDP dashboard, Click + *Create* and then select *Create eBook*.
3. **Kindle eBook Details tab**:
   a. **Language** – pick English or other language if needed.
   b. **Book Title and Subtitle** – Enter your title and subtitle *exactly* the same as you entered for your paperback so that both formats can be linked on Amazon once they are published.
   c. **Series** – Enter series name and number if needed.
   d. **Edition Number** – This is for a new edition of an existing book.
   e. **Author** – Enter your own name, or your pen name.
   f. **Contributors** – Enter any additional authors or contributors.
   g. **Description** – Enter your book description which can be the same as the description for your paperback.
   h. **Publishing Rights** –Click the option for "I own the copyright…".
   i. **Keywords** – Enter up to 7 keywords or keyword. They can the same as the ones for your paperback.
   j. **Categories** – Select up to 2 categories for your book. Refer back to the categories you selected during your pre-marketing research for Exercise 3c. in Step 3. Note: Categories are different for eBooks and paperbacks.
   k. **Age and Grade Range** – (Optional, use for children's book).
   l. **Preorder** – You have the option to setup a pre-order date ahead of time. Otherwise, select the *I am ready to release my book now* option. Note: It won't actually be live until you click *Publish* at the end.

Click **Save and Continue** at this point to continue to the next tab.

4. **Kindle eBook Content Tab:**
   a. **Manuscript**
      1) For the DRM option, I usually click Yes to Enable. Click the *How is my Kindle eBook effected by DRM* link to further information.
      2) Click *Upload* eBook *manuscript* and select your file. If you used Kindle Create, select the KPF file. Otherwise, refer back to the list of file types earlier in this chapter.

b. **Kindle eBook Cover** –Click the "Upload your cover file, and select the JPG for just the front cover of your book.

c. **Kindle eBook Preview** – Click *Launch Previewer* to preview your book. This may take a few minutes to load. In the Previewer, you can scroll through your pages to ensure that all pages look ok. If there are any issues, return to your manuscript to make any corrections, export your file and then return to re-upload your manuscript. To exit from the Previewer, click *Book Details* on the upper left.

d. **Kindle eBook ISBN** – Kindle eBooks are not required to have an ISBN. You have the option of adding one (which you would need to purchase). You also have the option of entering a Publisher imprint name. This can be a name that you create for your brand as a publisher.

Click **Save and Continue** at this point to continue to the next tab.

5. **Kindle eBook Pricing tab:**

a. **KDP Select Enrollment** – This allows you to run free promo deals and Kindle countdown deals, up to 5 days for each KDP enrollment period. Click the *Learn more* link for more information.

b. **Territories** - I usually pick All territories.

c. **Primary Marketplace** – Choose the location where you expect the majority of your book sales.

d. **Pricing and Royalty** – In this section, you can enter different prices to calculate your royalty, and decide on the best price for you book. To be eligible for the 70% royalty option, your eBook must meet the minimum price requirements, which is currently $2.99 at the time of writing this book. Once you enter the list price you would like to sell your eBook for, the estimated royalty amount displays. eBooks priced below $2.99 are eligible for the 35% royalty option.

e. **Book Lending** – This option allows customers to lend your eBook to family and friends for a duration of 14 days.

f. **Terms and Conditions** – Although it says to click publish to confirm that you agree with the terms and condition, ***DO NOT click the Publish Your Kindle eBook button until you are ready to*** *go live!!!* You may want to Publish your eBook in conjunction with the live date for your paperback. Click *Save as Draft* for now until you are ready to go live. Once you click the *Publish Your Kindle eBook* button, your eBook will be live within 72 hours.

Need more help with Kindle Direct Publishing and the Self-Publishing process? As part of the **Author Journey Success Toolkit** series, there is another book dedicated to this topic called **Self-Publishing Journey Success – How to Get Your Book on Amazon Using KDP**. Visit the Author Journey Success Series Toolkit Resources Page: https://ameliaswritingcorner.com/toolkit to learn more about this next book in the series.

You are almost there! Before you hit the Publish button, make sure you have everything you need to launch! This includes ordering the proof copy of your printed book, and a launch plan, which is covered in Step. 7.

Congratulations!

You have now reached the 6th milestone in your journey!

7

The Book Launch and Beyond

Step 7: The Book Launch and Beyond

The Launch Process

Now that you have uploaded your book files on KDP, here's a quick summary of things to do to prepare for your official go live and book launch:

- [ ] **Pick an official launch date.** Did you pick a launch date yet? If not, pick a launch date and stick to it! Clear your calendar for your launch date. Take the day off from work if possible and dedicate all or part of that day to promoting your book. You will need time to promote and celebrate!
- [ ] **Prepare your book mockups for promotional graphics**. There are many ways to create book mockups. Canva has lots of social media graphics that your can use to get started. Just add the front cover of your book to a ready-made template and download the graphics so they are ready to post on social media.
- [ ] **Contact your launch team**. In Step 4. you learned ways to network with other authors, which is one way to build a launch team; however, fellow authors may or may not be your ideal readers, so it's important to continue networking and reaching out to anyone you can think of who might be interested in your book. Remember to post about your book on online groups. Make a list of everyone, and then send them an email or message to let them know when your book will be available.
- [ ] **Review your paperback proof as soon as it arrives in the mail.** Did you receive your printed proof copy of the paperback version in the mail yet? Once your printed proof arrives, check your book inside and out. Check the front, spine and back cover as well as each and every page inside your book. If any changes are needed, update your files and re-upload them on KDP bookshelf. If you setup both a paperback and an eBook listing on KDP, remember you will need to convert and upload the interior of your manuscript for *both* versions. To upload any revised files, return to the *Bookshelf* tab on kdp.amazon.com; click *Continue setup* for each of your book listings (eBook and paperback) respectively, and navigate to the *Paperback Content* tab (for your paperback), or the eBook Content tab (for your eBook). As an alternative, you can click on the ellipses next to *Continue setup* to navigate directly to the content tab for each book

listing. On the corresponding tab, scroll down to the *Manuscript* and/or *Book Cover* section to re-upload your file(s). If the changes are very minor (like a small typo), you don't necessarily have to re-order a proof. However, if any major changes are made to your full cover or the interior, I would recommend ordering a proof to ensure the changes you made are correct and on point.

☐ **Confirm you book pricing.** Make sure the price for both your eBook and paperback are set to what you want for launch day on KDP. Consider running a free promo day for your eBook on launch. The KDP Select option allows you to run free promos or a countdown deal for your launch week. You can also manually change the price of your book at anytime on KDP Bookshelf. For either your eBook or Paperback, click on the ellipses and select the option to edit book pricing.

☐ **Write a launch day announcement.** Write one or more drafts for an announcement so you have it ready to post everywhere on social media. Don't just tell them to buy your book. Tell them what it's about and why they might like a copy.

☐ **Send an email to your email list.** If you already have an email list, send an email to your followers about your book launch. If you don't have an email list, start building one now. You can start First, create a freebie to share which could be a free chapter or blurb from your book, or even a list of tips (for nonfiction books) – you get the idea. Next, email everyone you know and offer the freebie, tell them about your book and ask them if you can add them to your email list. Consider signing up with MailChimp or another email program and setup a lead magnet page for your freebie.

Advanced Review Copy (ARC) Strategy

Remember the authors and potential readers you have been networking with along your writing journey? If you haven't contacted them yet, now is the time to contact them to ask if they might be interested in receiving a confidential, advanced review copy of your book for free. This may or may not result in an online review, but it will certainly help you share your book news and may help you improve your book content. Let your advanced reviewers know that any and all feedback is helpful. For the ARC file, I typically use a PDF version of my manuscript clearly marked as an "Advanced Review Copy". I also like to add the following, which is purely optional:

- Add the word "CONFIDENTIAL" in the file name when sent.
- Add a disclaimer at the beginning of the book, and/or in the email which states that it is the unofficial final version, and is for their private, confidential viewing and not to shared.

Some authors like to call this team of helpful readers a "Street Team" or "Launch Team". It's best to politely ask your reviewers to get back to you by a certain date, preferably a week or two before going live. This may help you with any last-minute editing and refining.

You can create a digital ARC in PDF, ePub, or Mobi format and distribute the ARC by emailing it directly to your readers, or through a website like NetGalley, BookFunnel, or Instafreebie. Microsoft Word and most software programs allow you to save directly to PDF format. To convert to ePub or Mobi format would require other tools like Calibre.

When your book is published, if you have an eBook version of your book (which I would highly recommended in addition to any print format), and if you use KDP for self-publishing your eBook, providing you have enrolled in KDP Select, you can setup a free promo day. This will allow your advanced reviewers to purchase your book for free so that they can leave a review on Amazon. Reviews during launch week are like gold! It works like this:

1. You send your PDF file (or other format) to your advanced readers a month or two before your book launch.
2. Your ARC team sends your feedback about what they like, don't like, or any other advice.
3. You publish your book on KDP and enroll in KDP Select, which allows you to setup a free promo day or days near or on your book launch date. Remember, if you picked June 1st as your "official" book launch date, you would need to publish your book a few days prior to make sure everything is in place for your launch (including your Look Inside feature, the linking of your eBook and paperback, and so forth). The Look Inside feature is usually automatic for eBooks, but you might have to contact KDP to setup the Look Inside for your paperback. Your eBook and

paperback should also automatically be linked under the same book listing on Amazon; however, if this does not occur automatically, you can contact KDP to inquire.

4. You let your advanced readers know when you your eBook will be free on Amazon (send them an email a few days prior and the day of). You can setup an email campaign in MailChimp for this purpose.

5. Your reviewers purchase your eBook for free on Amazon and leave you a review promptly.

6. During launch day and week, the goal is to have as many reviews as possible on Amazon which will help to boost your sales. Also, the more people who purchase your eBook, the more activity you will have for your book. The Amazon Algorithm loves sales activity and book activity, including organic searches. It's fine for you to send people your book link but encourage them to search for you book and tell them how to search.

Do a Soft Launch

While you are planning your official launch for your go live date, consider doing a soft launch. You can do a soft launch a few days or a few weeks ahead of time while you are waiting for your big day. Here are several things you can do during a soft launch:

☐ Do a cover reveal.

☐ Post about your book and tell everyone when it will be available.

☐ Update your author page, blog, and website with your book information.

☐ Add your book as a publication on LinkedIn.

☐ Tell everyone including your family, friends, co-workers, neighbors, etc. about your upcoming book.

☐ Have a launch day countdown (post each day, for 5 days leading up to your official launch day) using a fun promotional graphic.

☐ In general, get excited, be excited, and act excited about your book!

It's Time to Publish!

You have everything ready. Your book launch is coming soon. Your proof has been checked, and all systems are a go! Now it's time to return to KDP and click Publish! *See the Book Launch and Beyond chapter in the companion workbook for a Launch Plan Checklist.*

For your eBook:

1. Go to kdp.amazon.com and login to KDP by clicking on *Sign in*.
2. Make sure *Bookshelf* is selected at the top.
3. For your eBook, click the ellipses and select *Edit eBook Pricing*.
4. From the Kindle eBook Pricing tab, click *Publish Your Kindle eBook*.
5. It can take up to 72 hours for your eBook to be available on Amazon.

For your paperback:

1. Go to kdp.amazon.com and login to KDP by clicking on *Sign in*.
2. Make sure *Bookshelf* is selected at the top.
3. For your paperback, click the ellipses and select *Edit Print Book Pricing*.
4. From the *Paperback Rights and Pricing* tab, click *Publish Your Paperback Book*.
5. It can take up to 72 hours for your paperback to be available on Amazon.

Next, look for emails from KDP within 72 hours letting you know that your eBook and/or paperback book is now live and available for purchase!

I would recommend that you click the *Publish* buttons for both your eBook and paperback at least 5 days prior to your launch to ensure your book is ready for launch day. Once your eBook and paperback book are available, search for your book on Amazon using your name, book title, or ISBN. Check your book thumbnail, title, and book description to confirm that all information is correct. At that point, you are free to purchase a few copies of your very own book, directly from Amazon! This will not only give your book a boost in sales and ranking, but it will also give you an opportunity to test out the process and earn royalty. If you need to purchase more copies of your paperback, you can also purchase author copies through KDP at a reduced rate; from the KDP bookshelf, click *Order Author Copies*. Using this method, you only pay for the cost of printing, plus the cost of shipping. You do not earn royalties when you purchase author copies.

The Official Launch

It's launch day! You did it! Celebrate what you have done so far, and get ready to share your book with the world. This is the day to hustle and tell everyone you know that your book is live and available for purchase. Here's a list of things to do on launch day:

- ☐ Post your book announcement online everywhere (include a link on where to buy)
- ☐ Send an email to your email list to announce that your book is live
- ☐ Post mockup graphics of your book on your social media
- ☐ Ask for reviews
- ☐ Thank your followers, and ask them to purchase your book
- ☐ Send reminders about any upcoming events you may have set up (author expos, book fairs, book signings, etc.)
- ☐ Email any additional influencers (mentors, business colleagues, etc.), and ask them to share your book announcement post on their social media
- ☐ Update social media banners, headers, logos, etc. with your book (you can do this easily by adding a thumbnail of your book with a short blurb or tagline)
- ☐ Add a Buy Now button where applicable on your social media sites (for example, business Facebook pages allow you to have a Buy Now or Shop Now button – update this button with a link for your book)

Keep Promoting After Launching

Now that you have launched your book, it's important not to launch it and forget it. Instead, keep thinking of creative ways to promote your book. Consider throwing a post launch party. This can be online or in person. It can be as big or small as you like. Do something fun together. Depending on what you book is about, your launch party can be related to your book. Here are some ideas:

- ☐ If you wrote a cookbook, cook several recipes from your book and invite people over for a buffet.
- ☐ If you wrote a children's book, create a video of yourself reading part of the book (don't give it all away) and do a fun craft activity – then post this online and share away! You can also do this in person. Ask a local bookstore or library if you can have a book event – offer to donate part of the proceeds of your book sales to their organization.

- [ ] If you wrote a historical fiction or mystery novel, dress up like the main character and do a sample reading of your book – leave your audience in suspense!
- [ ] Just like when you buy a house and have a painting party, it takes real work after your launch to make sure your book flies. You can do it yourself or get others to help you fly your kite.

10 Simple Things To Do to Promote Your Book

1. **Treat Your Book Like a Baby** – Give your book lots of attention by displaying it proudly and announcing it to the world! Carry your book everywhere you go and show it to anyone you meet. Make visits to family and friends and show them your book. Be proud of your book!
2. **Create a Promotional Video** – Practice talking about your book and then when you are ready, go live on social media. You don't need a fancy camera – you can just use your mobile phone. Show your book and tell them something interesting about you or your book. Tell them why you wrote your book, how you wrote it, and what it's about. Consider filming this outside on a nice sunny day for good lighting.
3. **Create a Facebook Author Page or Fan Page** – Did you create an author page yet? Consider creating a business page on Facebook. Invite others, post about your book, and share information.
4. **Give Away a Chapter** – Save one chapter of your book in a PDF and offer it for free. Remember to include a call to action at the end of the free PDF, telling takers how they can purchase the whole book.
5. **Get Interviewed** – Contact other authors and ask them to interview you about your book. Post the interview on your author page or other social media.
6. **Contact Your Local Community Newspaper** – Ask your local community newspaper if they will do a story about you and your book.
7. **Ask For Reviews** – If you know someone who bought your book, ask them for a review. This can be an online review on Amazon or feedback they can send to you. Share their review on your social media.

8. **Write Another Book** – Have you considered writing another book? Depending on your genre, this can be a continuation of the story, or it can be a brand-new story with the same characters. If your book is nonfiction, consider a spin-off from your first book on a related topic. Post about your second book and get your audience engaged. Ask them what they would like to see in a second book while you get them interested in the first book!

9. **Update Your Email Signature** – Add a link to your book, author page, and social media in your email signature.

10. **Sign Up for an Author Expo** – Search online for book events, author expos, craft fairs or other events where you can sign up as a vendor to promote and sell your books.

Need more help with book promoting and marketing? Good news – there's another book in the **Author Journey Success Toolkit** series dedicated to this topic called **Book Marketing Success – 101 Ways to Promote Your Book**. Visit the Author Journey Success Series Toolkit Resources Page: https://ameliaswritingcorner.com/toolkit to learn more about this next book in the series.

Congratulations! You did it!

You have now reached the 7th milestone in your journey!

This is not the end of your journey, but just the beginning.

Resources

ISBN's

To purchase your own ISBNs, visit:
http://www.bowker.com/products/ISBN-US.html

Book Cover Templates:

KDP Book Template Download:
https://kdp.amazon.com/en_US/cover-templates

IngramSpark Book Template Download:
https://myaccount.ingramspark.com/Portal/Tools/CoverTemplateGenerator

Kindle Direct Publishing

KDP Main Website: https://kdp.amazon.com

KDP Supported eBook Formats:
https://kdp.amazon.com/en_US/help/topic/G200634390

Selecting Browse Categories:
https://kdp.amazon.com/en_US/help/topic/G200652170

Kindle Previewer (Screen shots, information and Download links):
https://www.amazon.com/gp/feature.html/?docId=1000765261

Kindle Previewer User Guide:
http://kindlepreviewer3.s3.amazonaws.com/UserGuide320_EN.pdf

Amazon Kindle Publishing Guidelines:
http://kindlegen.s3.amazonaws.com/AmazonKindlePublishingGuidelines.pdf

Paperback Manuscript Templates (Interior):
https://kdp.amazon.com/en_US/help/topic/G201834230

Kindle Create Download:

https://www.amazon.com/Kindle-Create/b?ie=UTF8&node=18292298011

Kindle Create Tutorial:

https://kdp.amazon.com/en_US/help/topic/GYVL2CASGU9ACFVU

How to Contact KDP:

1. Go to https://kdp.amazon.com/en_US/contact-us
2. Click on a category on left (Account, Getting Started, Format Your Book, etc.)
3. Click "Other" on the bottom left of the category.
4. Select an option on the right. Click "Send us an email" to send KDP a message with your questions; click "Call us" to receive a call back from KDP (your phone will ring, and you will be placed on hold until a representative is available to speak to you)

How to Download the Free Kindle for PC App

- Once purchased, the eBook version of this book will automatically download to your Kindle library on your iPhone, Android or other mobile device. To view this eBook on a computer (PC or MAC), while on your laptop of other computer, visit your country's Amazon site, and search for "kindle for pc". Follow directions to download the Kindle for PC app by selecting either PC Download or MAC download.
- If you are in Canada, see: www.amazon.ca/kindleapps for further information.

Need More Help?

If you have specific questions or need help with any step in this book, you can submit a question by using the *Contact Us* form on my blog. You can go to https://geni.us/askamelia or visit www.ameliaswritingcorner.com and then select *Contact Us* from the menu.

More Books in The Author Journey Success Toolkit Series

Get the Companion Workbook!

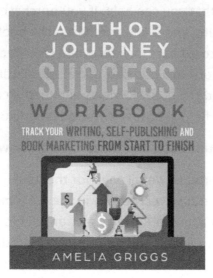

Learn More About KDP Inside and Out With Step-By-Step Guided Training

Learn 101 Ways to Successfully Market Your Book!

www.ameliaswritingcorner.com/toolkit

geni.us/authoramelia

How did you like this book?

Can you let me know what you found the most helpful in this book?

I understand that you may have purchased this book online or in a bookstore, so there are several ways that you can help. If you purchased the book online, leave a review on the website where you purchased the book. Online reviews help online rankings, which customers look for when they decide to make a purchase. If you purchased the book in a bookstore, consider letting the bookstore know how much you enjoyed the book. Reviews and feedback are so important and will truly help me provide more books like this one!

If you purchased this book on Amazon, here's how to post a review:

1. Go to the product detail page for the item.
2. Click *Write a customer review* in the *Customer Reviews* section. To get to the *Customer Reviews* section, click on existing reviews, or scroll down towards the bottom of the product page, and look for *Review this product*; then click Write a customer review. If you've placed an order for the item, you can also go to *Your Orders* and click *Write a product review*.
3. Select a Star Rating. A green check mark shows for successfully submitted ratings.
4. (Optional) Add photos, headline, or comments and click Submit.

If you purchased this book in person, please consider posting a review or rating on Amazon. I explain how in this video: geni.us/book-review

You can also find me on Instagram by searching for @ameliagwrites or go to: www.instagram.com/ameliagwrites

Send me a message or ask a question by using the Contact Us link on my blog. Just go to www.ameliaswritingcorner.com and click *Contact Us*.

Thank you in advance for your feedback!

Amelia

Made in the USA
Las Vegas, NV
19 February 2024

86000407R00083